A Prisoner's Love

by
Paul Taylor

Copyright © 2023 Paul Taylor

ISBN: 978-1-916820-83-8

All rights reserved, including the right to reproduce this book, or portions thereof in any form. No part of this text may be reproduced, transmitted, downloaded, decompiled, reverse engineered, or stored, in any form or introduced into any information storage and retrieval system, in any form or by any means, whether electronic or mechanical without the express written permission of the author.

PROLOGUE

EAST LONDON. THE YEAR WAS 1790.

SARAH and ROBERT who are brother and sister were ravenous. They saw the window of a house slightly ajar. ROBERT, who was aged 14, climbed through the window to see if he could find some food. Sarah who was just 16, protested to ROBERT not to do it but he was caught stealing. The police were called and both were arrested. At The Old Bailey Courthouse in London, ROBERT was sentenced to be hung. SARAH was sent to Australia to serve her prison sentence. That's where the adventure started. All alone and frightened, SARAH goes on to open an orphanage for children in Sydney Australia.

Paul Taylor's first book

THE RISE OF ESTHER
(based on a true story)

is available on Amazon.

ACKNOWLEDGMENTS

Scott Gaunt, my book cover designer.

Plus my friends for their help and encouragement:
Christine Todd
Darren Cooper
John Radley
Tracey Crossley
Katie Crowhurst.

A BIT ABOUT PAUL TAYLOR

Paul was born in Islington, north London. He went to Leycock school, north London. Paul married in 1969 to Linda. They have one son Nicholas who lives in Victoria, Australia.

Paul has always been a bit of a wheeler dealer sort of a chap, selling cement to branded trainers in London's famous chapel street market at the angel in Islington.

CHAPTER ONE

Times we're very hard in London's East End in 1790, especially for Sarah and Robert. Their father had passed away in a bad accident in the docks years earlier.

Robert aged 14 and Sarah aged 16 were sitting in the kitchen feeling cold and hungry.

Florence their mother was upstairs lying on her bed with flu. Both her and her children hadn't eaten any food for days. The cupboards were empty, any food that was in the house had been eaten days ago.

Florence calls down stairs " Make your selves something to eat kids", I am sure there is food in the kitchen."

Robert and Sarah looked at one another in dismay as they knew there was no food in the house.

Robert looked at Sarah, smiled called out to their mum, " Ok, mum don't worry we will both be ok , Sarah and I are going out for a walk to get some fresh air."

Florence calls back in a sickly tone, "ok, don't forget to take your key."

Sarah shouts up to her mum, " ok mum, love you lots". And out they both went.

Just ten minutes had passed, still in the back streets of the east end of London and by nowtheir hunger is now gnawing away at them, Robert points to a window of a housethat is slightly ajar. "Look Sarah there's a window open . I am sure I can climbthrough It and see if I can find us some food."

Sarah screams back at him, "No! Robert don't be silly you will get us into trouble, that is breaking and entering and against the law".
He screams back " we are both starving to death, mum as well. I know I can get in through that gap, it's no problem." Robert jumps up to the window ledge and climbs through the open window which leads into the kitchen.
"You stay outside Sarah because if I find some food I can pass it out the window to you."

Sarah is still protesting and tells Robert "our mum didn't bring us up to do this sort of thing." "I know Sarah but if we don't do something we will all starve to death."
Once Robert is inside the house Robert starts opening draws and cupboards looking for food. He finds a dish with half a used loaf of bread, some cheese and an old yellow cabbage.

He looks around the kitchen, and finds a large cloth and wraps the food into it.
Robert calls out to Sarah "Sarah come to the window I have found some food . I'll pass it through the window to you."
Robert turns and looks at the kitchen door as he hears someone coming. Robert freezes as the kitchen door is opened, There stood a tall rugged man who started shouting at Robert .
"What are you doing in my house.you thieving swine."
Robert is still holding the large cloth with the food in it,

Robert was frozen to the ground. The man entered the kitchen and knocks the food from Robert's hand the man then lunges towards Robert, holding Robert tightly around the chest. The man starts to shouts out loudly, "Help me help me, I have just caught a thief in my house".A man passing-by runs across the road and grabs Sarah around the neck pulling her to the ground and holds her till the police arrive .

Once inside the police station Robert and Sarah are separated and are put into different cells. They both told the same story about how they were starving and that Robert had only entered the house to find some food and were not interested in stealing anything else but food. They were both charged with house breaking and theft .

The next morning soon comes around they are both chained together by the ankles to prevent them from trying to escape. They were both taken outside the police station then put in to a horse driven wagon, with other prisoners going to the old Bailey court house for trail that day.

Poor Sarah cried all the way to the court house. Robert tried to lift his arm so he could comfort her. But the guard soon pulls Roberts arm down then slaps him hard around the head. The guard shouts at Robert so loudly it makes him jump "trythat again and I will break your nose, now sit down and keep still."

Robert and Sarah just looked at one another, both too frightened to move or speak..

The wagon stops outside the old Bailey court house. The guard pulls hard on the chains that are holding them together. The guard told them, "we are here, I'll get out off the wagon first, then you get out one at a time and follow me into the court house got it."

They both stood up and followed the guard walking slowly, with their heads hung low and in disgrace.

They both walk up the stairs into the court house it was a hive of activity. Men in long black cloaks were walking around every where holding stack's of papers under their arms. The noise was deafening, every one talking loudly like sparrows on a spring morning.

The guard took Robert and Sarah off to a side room, once inside the room he checked that their chains were secure and they could not escape and neither of them could run off. The guard looked at them then told them both, "I am going to book you in for your trail here today."

"You will be locked in this room for a short time before you go in front of the judge. So the pair of you sit on that wooden bench. I will find out who is representing you both and send him in to this room to speak with you. That will be the person who will represent you in your trial."

The guard turns, opens the door and locks it behind him. Sarah looks at Robert and shakes her head, "oh my god Robert I just can't believe what's happening to us. What about poor old mum, she will be worried out of her mind." Robert stares back at Sarah. "Don't worry Sis I think we will be all right. When the judge hears that wewere both starving, I am sure he will take pity on us It's not like we were stealing money or jewellery."

Sarah shrugs her shoulders. a guard opens the door and in front of them stooda man in a black gown." Good morning. My name is William Hutchings and I am going to represent you in the court room today. The judge that will be listening to your case is the Right Honourable Peter Ashby, I must warn you, he is a hard man that does not like people who break into houses, as his own house was onceburgled. I have read the police report .It seems it was only Robert that entered the house through an open window and his only Intention was to look for some food to eat as you were both starving. Is that correct? "Sarah speaks up, "that is correct sir."

    The man in the black cloak replies. "well as you were caught red handed on the property with the goods wrapped in a cloth I think you should plead guilty and lets pray the judge is in a good mood."Sarah asks, "and what if he is not in a good mood."
    The man in the black gown just hangs his head.he replies "GOD KNOWS." There is a loud knock on the door, and the sound of key's unlocking the door. The door slowly opens, a guard is standing there he calls to the man in the black cloak." You're up in 5 minutes sir, you're in court room two." The man in the cloak replies "ok, that's fine."

    Sarah grabs Roberts hand in fear of what's coming. She speaks to the man that is representing them. "Please sir will you get in touch with our mum and tell her what's happening to us. She is not well and does not know what's occurred."

    The man passes her some paper and a pencil," "write her name and address I will get someone from the court to contact her." Sarah gives the man a half smile and thanks him. The guard walks slowly back in to the room, ushering the three of them out of the room and up a corridor towards two big wooden doors with a sign above them stating court room two.

The guard knocks hard at the door. The door is then opened by a man on the other side.

All three of them walk into courtroom two. Robert and Sarah are told to stand in the wooden dock that's just in front of them. Their representative stands nearby.

A man in the court calls out "All be up standing for the judge". Every one stands as the judge enters the court room. The judge sits down and starts reading their case file which is before him on his desk.

The judge looks directly at Robert and Sarah and asks " How do you plead?" Their representative looks at the judge and says. "As these two where both caught red handed at the scene of the crime your honour I have advised them to plead Guilty, and not waste the time of the court and look for your leniency towards themespecially as they where only looking for some food to eat. They were starvinghungry and hadn't eaten in days. They would not of taken any money or jewellery from the house, only food my Lord."

The judge looks at both of them. "I have pre-read the papers on this case and although it is most unpleasant to be hungry, it is still not a good enough excuse to enter into a house. I appreciate the fact the window was slightly open. But In my opinion if Robert Wright had found some other goods including money or jewellery, he would have stolen that too. We must protect our property and goods at any cost . What makes you two think that you can just steal goods whether its money or food. People have worked hard for what they have you cannot just steal it from them just because you're hungry. What if they had no money to replace the food you stole , would that then give them the right to steal from someone because they were hungry. you disgust me ."

The judge continues.

"You young people must be taught a strong lesson and obey our laws.Robert Wright, even though you are just 14 years old, you know the difference between right and wrong." The judge puts on his black cap and speaks, "Robert Wright, you will be taken to Tyburn in London and hung by the neck until you are dead."

Robert collapses onto the floor screaming with fear. The judge stare's directly at Sarah Wright, "you did not enter the house and you did not handle the goods. Butyou could have walked away from this crime, but you didn't. So I am sentencing you to seven years in prison, not to be served in this country. Instead you will go by ship to our new continent called Australia. Now take them both away and out of my sight ." Two guards lift Robert from the floor and to his feet. Robert screamed out to the judge, " please don't hang me sir, I was only looking for something to eat."

Sarah also screamed out to the judge " Please judge. Don't do this. My brother is only 14 years of age.For god's sake, please show us some pity. We were both starving to death." The judge stands up and turns away from Robert and Sarah then walks through a door that's behind his seat and leaves the court room .

Sarah is handcuffed to one guard whilst Robert is to another. Both of them in utter shock as to their fate. Once they were at the bottom of the stairs, Robert was dragged one way, whilst Sarah another way.Sarah screams out to Robert. "I love you Rob." Poor Robert who was crying so loudly responds, "and I love you too sis, please tell mum I

7

am sorry and I love her." They went their separate ways never to see one another again.

CHAPTER TWO

The journey to Australia

Sarah Wright is in a large open wooden wagon with lots of other women prisoners, all of them are chained together by the ankles. Their chances of escaping were zero.The mood was very solemn. As all the prisoners depart from the wagon, in front of them was a huge sailing ship, with lots of people loading goods onto the ship. They were loading everything on board like flour, fruit, potatoes, drinking water, chickens, and a couple of cows for their milk plus goods for the sick bay and much moreto help them cross the oceans on their journey to the other side of the world . The women prisoners are in a long line waiting to walk slowly up the gangplank and on to the ship. To start their journey to the unknown world as far as they were concerned.

An officer of the Marines was counting the prisoners on board, one by one he was ticking them of off his list. Whilst another officer writes down the names checking that every prisoner is accounted for.

Once on board a marine directs the women prisoners down the steep wooden steps leading to the cells below.After some time all the women prisoners are on board the ship. A marine officer calls out to all the women prisoner's, "Okay, ladies. Remove all your clothing and be smart about it."

The women prisoners look at each other wondering what was coming next but after a minute or so they all start to strip off their tattered rags that by now you couldn't recognise as clothing. Just dirty smelly rags.

A marine offer called out again, "look behind you. You'll see some troughs with soap and water in them."So ladies wash yourselves down starting with your hair, your face, your body and legs. And ladies please wash your private parts too".When you have finished, if you look to the side of you, you will see some clean cloth to dry yourself with. Then if you look behind you, you will see a rack with some nice clean prison uniforms for you to wear.

These uniforms must be kept clean at all times. Next week you will be given another clean set to wear. Your dirty uniform must be washed by you and saved ready to wear the following week.

If any of you have an accident and stain your uniform you must report it straight away. If you do not adhere to these rules you will be severely punished, we will not have messy or dirty prisoners aboard this ship.

Also ladies you must clean and scrub out your cells so they look brand new every day if necessary, we do an inspection. Every two weeks you will get fresh clean bedding that once again must be looked after at all times. If you have an accident with your bedding, once again you must report this straight away so the problem can be dealt with. Failing to do this will result in harsh punishment , and let me tell you that's something you want to avoid."

The mood changes for most of the women prisoners even those hardened prisoners that have been in Newgate jail for some time.most of the women prisoners just strip off their clothes. They were not shy some women are screaming out laughing and jumping up and down for joy.

A woman prisoner by the name of Claire Marchant looks at Sarah and can see that she is struggling to remove all her clothes in front of the other prisoners.

Claire asks Sarah," are you okay sweetheart." Sarah replies," not really" Claireasks Sarah, "what's your name." She replies, "my name is Sarah, what's yours," oh my name is "Claire ."

Claire asks, " have you got a problem with removing your clothes in front of others."
She replies in a quiet shy why, "what do you mean." "What I mean is Sarah do you have a problem stripping off your clothing in front of other women prisoners"."To be honest Claire I do. I come from a small family in East London, I didn't have a dadjust a younger brother, and on bath night's we would strip off our clothing in privatebefore getting into our tin bath".

I know that I am 16 but nobody has ever seen my naked body. So you can imagine how I feel stripping off completely naked not only in front of the other women prisoners but the male marines as well.""I know Sarah, but you're just going to have to get used to it. Or the guards will start to pick on you. They might even punish you in some way, I'll tell you what I'll stand in front of you. Then you can strip off your clothes get a wash down, grab a uniform and get yourself dressed. How's that." Then not too many people will notice you.

Getting herself washed quickly and dressed in her prison uniform. Sarahsaid" Thank you for your kindness Claire I will not forget that." "That's alright darling, I don't mind showing my body, in fact I am quite proud of my breasts. Well my boyfriend used to like them." Both women start laughing.

A guard shouts out loud to all the women prisoners ," ok listen up you lot", now you have all had a wash down and put your uniforms on, I want you all to stand in a straight line against the back wall so I can work out what cells I want you to go into.

An Irish lady walks up and stands next to Claire and Sarah. She looks at both of them and speaks, "hello girls my name is Maria . Can I stand next to you two, then hope fully we can share a cell together. I heard you two laughing so I would rather be in a cell with people that have a sense of humour. Most of the other women look like a load of miserable cows. That would be like torture being banged up with them for maybe six months or so."

Both Sarah and Claire smile at Maria, Claire says. "That will be fine as long as you don't snore".Maria "sorry girls I don't know if I snore, once I am asleep then I am sleep." plus I can't hear myself once I am a sleep.

All three women start to laugh," An officer calls out to the women prisoner's. "Ok you lot" keep the noise down and listen to me Iwant you to stand in a straight line next to the cell and as I walk along I will gather you in lots of three to go into the cell behind you."

"So just listen to me and do as you are told".When the officer got to Claire, Sarah, and Maria, he just opened the cell door and all three women walked in, the door being slammed hard behind them.

Maria speaks first, "oh well ladies that worked out ok." All three women look around the cell, there was a strong smell of tar as the walls had been coated with it. The floor was polished wooden boards , three bunk beds, with no pillows but one blanket per bunk bed also a wooden bucket for their waste.

Maria asks, "well ladies please choose a bunk or do we just sit down on the one that we are standing next to."All the women just sat down on a bunk, Claire spoke first, "well let me introduce my self, my name is Claire, and how I got here was one night I went out to have a beer or two with some of my girl friends when some man walked over to me and called me an old slut . Well I did no more than hit him over the head with a beer bottle .I told the judge what the man had said to me, plus I was a little drunk, but he still gave me seven years to be served in this unknown place called Australia or something like that."

"Well girls, my name is Maria Connolly I am originally from Dublin, I came to London with my, boyfriend. Who after a few months decided to go back to Dublin and I am here because well lets put it this way I was fitted up by the

Governor of the house where I worked as a live-in house keeper. I had a nice little room in the house and one night, whilst his wife and children were away at their summer house in Kent, the Governor came up to my room and stayed the night.

This went on for about six weeks or so .He even told me he loved me and as a fool I believed him. One day he brought me a lovely brooch. To be honest it felt good and I liked him.

He told me one day that his wife was returning home from Kent with the children and our fling had to stop. Me being silly I had fallen in love with him, especially as he had told me that he loved me too. Well I told him he would have to tell his wife the truth about us as we were in love, or so I thought.

I have never seen some one so frightened he went as white as a ghost, thenstormed out of the room swearing and shouting. The next thing I knew the law hadcome to the house and were searching my room. He had told the coppers that a brooch was missing. And yes they found the brooch in my room, the same one he had bought for me. And that was that, as they say. I was nicked for stealing the brooch and out the way before his wife and children got home."

Claire calls out to Maria, "what a bastard" Maria says " I know. The dirty git. He stitched me up good and proper. I went in front of the judge at the old Bailey and I got ten years in this place called Australia."

As Sarah was listening to all of this she just couldn't hold back the tears any more. and started crying inconsolably. Claire went over to her bunk, put her arm around her shoulders and Sarah wiped her eyes with the blanket that was on the bed.

Sarah starts to tell her story. "Me and my younger brother were so hungry. We hadn't eaten for a few days. We didn't have a dad and our mum was upstairs in bed feeling unwell. So me and my little brother went out for a walk around the streets of East London where we lived. As we were walking along , my brother saw an open window of a house . Before I knew it , Robert had jumped up and squeezed through the gap. Girls, I promise he was only looking for some food for us to eat. He opened a cupboard and found some bread, cheese and an old cabbage. He grabbed them and wrapped them in a cloth that was on the table.

That's when a man came into the room and grabbed poor Robert. The man was screaming out for help . I started screaming back at the man to let my brother go. Then a man passing by in the street came running over and grabbed me. The law came and they threw us both into jail. The next day Robert and me where put in a wooden wagon with other prisoners and driven up to the old Bailey. A man was appointed to help us, he told us because we were caught bang to rights at the scene he advised us both to plead guilty and hoped the judge would show some mercy on us ."

.

Maria asks, "and did the judge show any mercy." "no not at all" Sarah cries out . She starts crying uncontrollably again. Claire still with her arm around

Sarah's shoulder, hugs her tightly. "No the judge showed no pity on us he sentencedRobert to be hung at the TYBURN GALLOWS in London."

Claire and Maria both screamed out at the same time. "Oh no hung , what your little brother". "Yes, they took my little brother away and hung him two weeks later.""The judge told me as you did not enter the house or touch the goods he would sentence me to seven years to be served like you in Australia."

"Maria, It seems impossible that they could take a young child and hang him. All the poor boy wanted was some food, I hope the judge rots in hell."

Claire also agrees, " that's bloody terrible I think that's the worst story I have ever heard". A guard walks along the corridor of the ship where all the prisoner's are held in their cells, a flap on the door slides across and the guard peers into the cell"okay you lot turn the candle out get to sleep you'll get another knock on the door in the morning". Each girl agrees it's been a long day and they might as well get their head down for the night. They snuggle into their bunks pulling the blanket over them. They say their good nights and slowly they all drop off to sleep.

The next morning there's a loud bang on the cell door a guard shouts out, "come on every one get up",The women slip into their uniforms then they walk out into the corridor. The women prisoners from every other cell are getting out of their bunks, put their uniforms on and come out of their cells also into the ships corridor.

A guard called out to all of them, "ok you lot I want you to walk over to that table opposite. Every morning I need you to take off your uniform and get yourselves thoroughly washed and I mean a thorough good wash down and not a cats lick."

"Once you have done that, at the end of the corridor you'll find a table with food and water I want you to take your food and water back to your cells. When you haveeaten your food you have to bring your plate and cup back where you can wash and dry them ready for later."

Once back inside the cell they all sat down on their bunks and started eating there food . Claire speaks "blimey girls I didn't know this was going to be a five star trip."All three women start to laugh. Once they had finished their food and drink they made their bunks up all nice a tidy. Then one by one walked out of the cell back into the corridor to a place where they washed and dried their plates and cutleryand put them away.

All the women prisoners were standing around in the corridor awaiting their next order. There were by now lots of guards walking around them, some were looking them up and down in a mischievous manner . One cocky guard walks into the crowd of women squeezing their breasts and bottoms. Some of the women prisoners were laughing, whilst others didn't like it but where too frightened to say anything for fear that they might get beaten by the guards.

The cocky guard walked over to Claire and grabs her bottom, "cor you got a nice little bottom, what's your tits like". He tries to grab her breast Claire gives out one big scream, "Fuck off you ugly bastard. I wouldn't want you even if you had diamonds hanging on it." Most of the women prisoner's went quiet, but the other guards all started laughing at the cocky guard, and mocking him.

He replies, "you cheeky cow, you'll find out if it's got diamonds on it or not."The guards are by now all fired up, some laughing some willing the cocky guard on calling out, "go on show the bitch what you got."

The cocky guard grabs Claire around the neck and starts dragging her into a cell to have sex with her.

All though totally out of character Sarah jumps at the cocky guard and starts punching him in the face. "Leave her alone, just leave her alone"She calls out, "Ain't it bad enough that we are herded around like cattle on this fucking ship let alone someone like you picking on us and trying to make our lives hard you're a coward and a bully."

"Ok" says the cocky guard, "you want to play it rough do you ya, well I'll show you how to play it rough." He grabs out at Sarah holding her around the neck and starts pulling her into the cell. Sarah tried to resist, but with no luck, he was too strong. She started to wriggle free he punches her in the face and throws her to the floor punching her again in the face . Blood starts pouring out of her mouth. All the other guards are laughing thinking it's funny at what's happening to poor Sarah.

A lot of women prisoners were protesting and screaming out loud hoping he would stop. But the cocky guard just carried on and throws Sarah onto one off the bunks and starts tearing at her clothing, her uniform rips, the guard is now out of control as he climbs on top of her trying to kiss the side of her face. Poor Sarah is screaming and still trying to fight him off but she is pinned down and losing her strength .

An officer of the marines is walking on the top deck near to the stairs that leads down to the cells. His attention is drawn by the noise coming from cells area.. He comes down the stairs to the cells where everyone is gathered around including prisoners and guards .

The marine officer pushes his way through the crowds of prisoners to the entrance of the cell door where he can see exactly what going on.

He draws his sword and with the flat side off his sword the officer hits the guard on his back, not holding back on how hard he hits him .The guard jumps back in pain rolling off of Sarah instantly and falling to the floor. The officer then putsthe tip of his sword into his throat, The guards eyes are so far open with fear and pain from the crashing blow of the sword, but he was too frightened to utter a word, he just lay there in utter shock that he had been caught.

Sarah tried to stand but falls onto the floor, The blood from her face was everywhere, her uniform was also torn and bloody. "What's goi ng on here," screams the officer, "Well sir, she started playing up, I tried pushing her back into the cell and a accidentally fell on top of her."

All the woman prisoners started screaming out , "no that's not true he was trying to rape her." Claire stepped forward, "yes sir that's right, he started on me first grabbing me around the neck and trying to pull me into the cell. He was trying his hardest to rape me .

I screamed at him to leave me alone. He started on me, if you hadn't come along god know's what would have happened".

The officer said, "Thats what it looked like to me, so get up you bastard you're under arrest." He turns to the other guards, and say's, " if I find that any other of you were involved in this you too will be arrested and punished". He then points to two of the guards, "take the prisoner down to the bowels of the ship, put him in irons and throw him into a cell.

The rest of you back to your cells and be smart about it as for you guards if I hear of any more disruption down hear you all will be on a charge, Got it". The guards all seemed to called out at the same time. "Yes sir."

The marine officer calls two guards over, " take this women prisoner to the sick bay, tell the doctor what's happened, and tell him I'll be down later to get a report on how she is getting on".

The guards helped poor Sarah to her feet, she staggered off with them one each side supporting her .,Other women prisoners gathered at their cell doors just watching Sarah being helped away battered and bruised.

CHAPTER 3

THE PUNISHMENT

Early the next morning all the ship's crew, marines and officers, plus the captain of the ship were on the top deck to witness the flogging of the male guard.

The crew stood on one side of the ship whilst the marines stood the other side facing each another. The officers and captain stood in the middle.two guards brought the prisoner up the wooden stairs which led to the top deck ready for his punishment. The guards led him to a wooden hand rail where they undid the irons that were around his hands and tied his wrists with rope to the hand rail so he couldn't move.

A marine walked over and stood behind the prisoner and was waiting for the officers command.
First the officer called out to all the crew, " Marines, guards, and crew, you have allbeen brought here today to bare witness to the flogging of George Taylor, a guard who thought he could take advantage of a woman prisoner. He beat her, punched her and tried to take sexual advantage of her. A woman prisoner that couldn't fight back in my opinion he is a coward and a disgrace. And someone who has tried to take advantage of his position.

I need you to watch the punishment so you will know what to expect should you have it in your mind to do the same as this man has done, even though at some point

you might even get encouraged by a women prisoner who would always want a favour in return."
.

The officer calls out this time even louder, "do you all understand me?". "Yes sir we do", they shouted back, all of them with a stern face.

The officer calls out to the marine, "let the punishment begin." The marine steps forward picks up the leather whip which had metal studs attached to it. The studs would cut deep into the skin and scar a man's back for life.The officer instructs the marine, "give this man fifty of your best strokes". The marine lifts his hand holding the whip tightly then thrusting the whip forwards and striking the prisoners back with the leather lashes .

He screams out with the pain of the studs cutting hard and deep into theflesh of his back. Fifty strokes later and the prisoner is now unconscious. Theguards cut the prisoner's hands free. His Body falls on to the deck. Blood is pouring from the raw flesh on his back. One of the guards has a bucket of seawater ready, he throws it over the prisoner's back, blood flows everywhere.One member of the crew fainted, several others where sick .

The prisoner starts to come round, his lifeless body is still laying on the deck of the ship. Two guards walk forwards pulling him to his feet. The prisoner is screaming in agony as he is dragged off the floor and put back down in his cell below decks in the bowel of the ship.

The officer calls out to everyone, "you have witnessed the punishment to this wicked man and this punishment will be delivered to any man on this ship if they don't follow the rules of the ship, especially where the prisoner's are evolved.

That stands for both crew and marines alike, so please remember this day before you ever get tempted. You are now all dismissed, go back to work all of you."All the men walk off to do their Jobs aboard the ship , most of the men remain quiet.

The marine officer turns and speaks to the captain, " I don't think we will have any more problems like that again".The captain replies, " I hope not, that was despicable, what that man tried to do to that poor girl ."

"The things that men try to do, If he had raped her I think the only sentence would have been to hang the man." "I totally agree with you captain." Both men salute to each other then go their separate ways. The marine officer walks down the wooden stairs to the sickbay where Sarah's is lying on her back.

The officer firstly walks up to the doctor and asks, "Doctor may i ask how the young girl is that was brought down to the sick bay yesterday." The doctor replies, "I have cleaned her up. She is badly bruised around the body and head so I would like to keep her in the sick bay for around six or seven days so I can keep a close eye on her in case of concussion or internal bleeding."

"That's fine," replies the officer, "please let me know if there's any change in her condition." The doctor replies, "I will report to you if there are any changes in her."

The officer walks back up the stairs to the top deck walking around slowly observing what the crew and his marines are doing.

CHAPTER FOUR

DOWN IN THE SICKBAY

The next day in the sickbay Sarah woke up early, she was the only patient in there, the doctor was in his own little room asleep. Sarah sat up and rubbed her head that was still feeding sore. Looking around the sickbay she thought to herself it looksvery clean but very untidy, boxes of tablets here, medicines there, and bandageslying everywhere all different sizes. She thought what a mess, I wonder if he has a nurse that helps him.

Sarah hears some noise and looks around to see the doctor walking towards her.
"Good morning Sarah,I am glad to see you awake, you were out for the count yesterday."She nodded, "I know sir." He asks, "I would like to do a few tests on you, ok." She smiles back at him, "what kind of tests do you have in mind sir?"
"Oh don't worry I am not going to cut you open or anything like that". Sarah replies quickly, "thank god for that sir, I was getting worried for a moment"

The doctor looks into her eyes, "right move your eyes to the left, now to the right, that's good ok, I am going to put my finger in front of your eyes, Please let your eyes follow my fingers as I move my hand, that's it your doing fine.He tells her as she follows his finger. Now Sarah please lay down, I am sorry to have to do this after your all ordeal, but I would like to check your body over to look at your bruises and your limbs to see if you have any fractures or broken bones."

She lies back into her bunk the doctor gently puts his hands on her head examining it, "ok I am going to put some iodine on these cuts. It will sting but it will help to keep them clean and stop any infection".

The doctor walks over to a large cupboard opens a bottle of iodine & pours some on to a soft clean cloth and dabs onto Sarah's cuts. She jumps up and says,"oh boy doc that stings" He replies, as " I told you it will clean the cuts and stop you getting any infections". Sarah lies back down again. The doctor starts moving from cut to cut.He tells Sarah, "right thats the cuts sorted out now let me examine your bones." He moves his hands gently across her arms and legs, feeling for any brakes.

"That's good Sarah, I can't find any broken bones , so i think it's just rest and take it easy for three or four days." She smiles and thanks the doctor.The doctor walks back to a table puts the cloth and bottle down, he turns to Sarah "I am going to get some food and some fresh water, shall I bring some back for you?","Yes please sir." The doctor walks up the wooden stairway to the top deck and returns about five minutes later with a tray full of food and a jug of water. He asks Sarah, "would you like to get up to sit with me and eat some food?" She nods, her head"Yes please sir ."

Sarah slowly gets off of her bunk, sits opposite the doctor and they munch into there food .The Doctor asks her "so how did a pretty girl like you wind up on a prisoner ship?"Sarah tells the doctor the whole story from beginning to the end, telling him about Roberts fate. He say "my god that's terrible, what you have told me must seem like a horrible dream." "Yes, that's right doctor a dream that I can't seem towake up from .

She looks down at the floor and starts to cry. He says,"but at least you're here to tell the tale. I wish my brother Robert was here too." By the way Sarah, "my Christianname is Peter so if there's no one around please call me Peter or doctor. If others are present you must call me Sir, as that's the rules of the ship" "Oh. you're so kind Peter , may I ask you a question." He replies "please go ahead." "Well I have always dreamed of one day becoming a nurse. I hope you don't mind me saying but I have had a look around your surgery and although it's very clean it don't look very organised as there are bandages here and there, different medicine scattered about. I might be wrong Peter but it all seems a bit of a muddle".

"So what are suggesting", "well I would love to work down here with you as yourassistant and you could train me in medical ways leading to me becoming a nurse. That way when we get to Australia I can help people as a nurse in the prison hospital. I am not looking for an easy ride, I genuinely would like to train as a nurse. Peter if I am not any help to you or you think I am lazy just send me back to my cell."

He thinks for a moment, "it is a good idea as I am running the surgery on my own and if I had two or three patients it could get difficult, but I would have to getpermission from the ship's captain and he might not like that idea."

"Peter, although I feel bruised and sore please can I get up and may be have a little tidyup say start with the bandages."Peter smiles at her, "well you are keen but Sarah please keep all the bandages together in sizes, that would be a big help."

She smiles at him," I promise I will keep them all together in the correct sizes nice and tidy so you will know exactly where they are.""That's the idea, I need to go up to the top deck and do my inspection of the prisoners below and Sarah if you come over faint or tired, just rest". "Ok" Sarah replied. Doctor Peter walks up the wooden stairs that lead to the top deck & then on his way to do his rounds and check out all the women prisoners

Sarah starts to tidy up all the bandages, getting them into their right sizes, there areso many but Sarah gets them all together nice and neat ready for use. Doctor Peter returns, he looks at Sarah and smiles, "well done, that's a very good job you have done, I didn't realise what a muddle they were in ."

At that moment a couple of Guards walk into the sickbay holding up a sailor who had badly cut his hand open. Blood was dripping everywhere.Doctor Peter quickly calls the sailor over and sits him down then starts to inspect his hand.
He calls over to Sarah, "bring me over that bucket of clean salty water so I can clean this mans' cut hand and see what's going on." Peter pushes his hand into the water and tries to wash the wound over to make sure there was nothing inside the cut that could get infected.

He lifts the sailors hand from the water and inspects it. It's still bleeding badly.

"Erm that's a deep cut", He tells the sailor. "Sarah if you look in the cupboard below the bandages you will find a box of twine a needle and some thick bandages, bring them over to me and put them on the table in front of me".

She does as she is told quickly and efficiently, "ok Sarah, I need you to hold the sailors hand with your left hand and with your right squeeze the veins on his wrists as hard as you can to try to stop the blood as it is still falling everywhere onto the floor and on your hands".

The doctor tips some spirit from a bottle onto the sailor's hand, The sailor shouts out,"bloody hell doc that stings," the doctor replies, "I know, but it will clean the wound."

Sarah is still holding the man's hand and wrist blood has now started to slow down, Dr Peter picks up his needle and twine that he had threaded and starts to sew theskin together. Sarah is holding the sailors hand and wrist very tightly, Doctor Peter looks at her and thinks, "you are doing a grand job", He then tells her.

Sarah looks at the doctor, she smiles, then thanks him, "thank you sir". He asked Sarah to rest the man's hand on the table, pick up the bandage and hand it to him, which she does. Dr Peter bandages the sailors hand and puts it in a sling. He then tells the sailor, you mustn't work for at least 14 days but I need to see you in five days to check the wound and re-dress it. The sailor thanks the doctor and the nurse for their help and leaves the surgery.

The doctor tells Sarah, "well done, I am very pleased with you, That was a very good test as I didn't know how you would react to all that blood but you certainly passed the test, well done."

"Thank you Peter and I even remembered to call you sir", both start laughing, Sarah tells Peter' "when I was young I used to watch my mum, she wasn't medically trained but a lot of our friends and neighbours would come around to our house and my mum would sort them out, because none of them had any money to pay a doctor." I think she learnt by watching her mum .

She says. "I'll get some clean water, some carbolic soap and wash all this blood from everywhere' including ourselves".
Peter thanks her, "yes and I had better write a report on this man's hand and enter it in to our log."
The very next morning Peter asks Sarah , "are you serious about working with me in the sick bay because you will see some horrible things and maybe even peopledying in front of you. That's a lot to take in for a young person."

She replies, "please Sir, let me work in here with you and I promise I will never let you down. My young brother was only14 and hung. He stole some bread and some cheese because my mum was sick and we were starving. I can't get him out of my mind, the hard work in the sickbay will certainly help me a lot."

Dr Peter replies, "okay let me have a word with the Captain and the officer of the marines to see what they think about the idea of you working and helping here.Thank you Peter," she replies, Peter tells Sarah, "To be honest I just don't know how I would get on if a lot of the crew all got sick all once "and to be frank it worries me, he said looking at Sarah with a worried look on his face. "You know what , I am going to see the captain right now." Up the wooden stairs he thumped determined to talk to the captain about how he would like to train Sarah as his nurse.

Peter walks the length of the ship where he sees the captain talking to the officer of the marines.
"Good morning gentlemen and how are you both on this fine morning", they both turn and smile at the doctor. "Yes we are both fine," they reply, "is all well with you doctor," yes thanks, but there is something that I would like to talk to you about".
The captain asks him, "ok, is now a good time," Doctor Peter replies, "yes now is good a good time as any I would like to ask you both a question." the officer says, " fire away Doctor.If we can help you we surely will". "Well gentlemen, It has been worrying me a little, If more than one of the crew or marines becomes sick I would have a problem looking after them at the same time specially in an emergency.

We had member of your crew in the sickbay with a very deep cut to his hand, Luckily I had a woman prisoner who has a little bit of knowledge help me sort the poor man out. After speaking to her, she would like to work with me in the sickbay. I could train her to become a very good nurse. I have told her I would have to get permission from you both before I could even consider it. To be honest it does make sense."The marine officer told him.

The captain looked at the officer' "well yes, I suppose it does ,what do think," He asks the officer.

The officer replies with a stern face, "providing you take full responsibility for her and it's recorded in the ships Log book it will be ok with me, but there can be no wandering around the ship unless you are with her, do you understand? "."Doctor Peter replies " Ii do understand and I totally agree."

The officer asks, "is that the woman prisoner that got beaten up that helped you? ". "Yes it is".The officer smiled then replied, "oh well that's good hopefully she's on the mend".

He thanked them both and returned to the sickbay to give Sarah the news.He explained to her that they had agreed but you must not walk out of the sickbay on your own at any time unless you are with me or you will be sent back to your cell for the rest of the Journey too Australia." Do you understand that rule?" Sarah nodded her head then thanked Peter and told him "I promise I will not let you down".

Doctor Peter says to Sarah, "If you come with me there's a small but comfortable room with your own bunk and table at the other end of the sickbay where you can put any bits that you might have".She laughs, "Peter, I have nothing only the uniform I stand in." She looks around the small room and smiles with glee thinking to herself, I have never in my whole life had my own room.

"Peter you have been so kind to me," she leans forward and without thinking kisses him on the side of his face, "Oops' l am so sorry she tells him." Peter firstly goes red in the face , he then smiles at her then tells her , "well that's the nicest thank you I have ever had." They both saw the funny side of it and started to laugh.

CHAPTER 5

EVERY DAY LIFE IN THE SICKBAY

Sarah settled nicely into her everyday life in the sickbay. She worked hard andorganised everything into all its little homes from bandages to bottles of drugs.
It was all nicely washed, cleaned and put away neatly. Peter was so pleasedwith her work. Even the captain and the first officer commented on how well she was doing and how clean and efficiently the sickbay was running, although so far they had only treated small or minor injuries.

One day Sarah asked Peter, "tell me if you don't mind, what is your surname?"
He tells her with a smile on his face, "Well it's KINGSWOOD", "why do you ask?"
"I don't know I am just curious."
"Peter what sent you on this journey to Australia?" "Well when I saw the job advertised in a medical journal, it got my juices flowing. I thought to myself a new start a new continent it was just what I was looking for. I was working in a hospital in the north of England and I thought to myself I am a young man with new ideas but I could see myself getting stuck in a rut just like my father, who is also a doctor".

So I thought why not both my parents were very sad that I took this job as it is so far away and when I left I did think to myself will I ever see them again.

But my brother gave me great encouragement. He told me, "Peter if you ever have enough of Australia you can always get on a ship and come back, but you don't want to go through life thinking what if." So here I am on a new adventure." Australia here I come . But I have promised myself that I will write to my parents and my brother each month.

A couple of months have now passed, a bad storm is underway, an injured sailor isbought down to the sickbay by two other sailors.
Doctor Peter asks one of the sailors that bought him down, "what's happened to this man."
"He has had a bad fall sir. He was in the rigging trying to cut down a sail that had torn in half , but the wind was just too strong. He must have lost his grip then andfell on to the deck."
He instructs the men to lay him on the table that was in front of them and calls out to Sarah, "get me a bucket of clean water please." She replies "yes sir," and brings it back to the table where the poor man is laying. The doctor starts washing the blood from the sailor's head so he can see how bad his injuries are.
The injured sailor opens his eyes for a few seconds looking directly at Sarah and then Peter, his eyes close and he takes his last breath. The doctor looks at his chest to see if he is breathing, and checks his pulse for a heartbeat but there is nothing no pulse what so ever.
Peter stands up straight tells Sarah and the two guards, "sorry this man has died of his injuries."

The two sailors look at one another. Sarah sheds a little tear, thinking of her little brother. One of the sailor's asks, "is there anything else we can do doctor before we go back to work." He replies "my nurse and I will deal with the body but I need yournames to go into my Log." They do this and leave.

Sarah asks the doctor," is there nothing we can do for this poor man?" "No, I am sorry Sarah. "This poor man has passed away. i must write a report on him and the accident that brought him to his death."

"Sarah will you please remove this man's clothing? You can just cut them off. We need to clean up his body. We then wrap him in a white sheet ready to be buried at sea. This is something we have to do as we cannot store the body."

Sarah looks at the lifeless body and starts to weep, Peter walks over to her and puts his arm around her. "What's wrong Sarah, are you sad because this is the first dead body you have encountered?"
She replies, "no it's not that, my mind had a flash back and thoughts of my dead brother came into my mind." And his poor dead body after he had been hung.
Peter puts his arms around her, holding her tight making her feel safe, a few tears were still rolling down her checks. He releases his bear hug type grip, then raises his hand and wipes away the tears with his finger. She looks directly into his eyes, moves her head slightly forward. He does the same, their lips meet and they kiss but this time in a very passionate way it takes them by both by surprise.

Sarah pulls her head away, " oh I am so sorry I don't know what came over me. I feel that I have tried to take advantage of your kindness towards me." Peter looks at

Sarah, smiles at her and replies, "Sarah I have been wanting to do that for some time now."

"She lunge's her head forwards again and both her and Peter embrace with such passion."

Sarah tells him "that is the first time in my whole life that I have kissed anyone otherthan my dear old mum and my little brother." He smiled back at her, "well to be honest I have no experience in kissing ever. All I know is that kissing you was incredible. Please don't think that I'm being silly but I think I have fallen in love with you."

Her face lit up, she kisses him gently on the side of his face and replies with a big smile, "Peter I feel the same about you , but I didn't know how to tell you."

He tells her, "you don't know how happy that makes me feel, but we haveto be careful not ever to show our feelings for each other in front of anybody as I could lose my job and you could be sent back to your cell."

"Please don't worry about me, I will never betray your trust. Tell me how could I betray the man I love."
Peter once again looks at Sarah and thanks her. He tells her, "I am so happy that we both feel the same way about each other. It has been going over and over in my mind I just didn't know how to tell you."
She tells him, "how could any women not fall in love with you you're such aKind caring man and so nice to be around."

A little later that day, the door opens to the sickbay, both the captain and the first officer walk in, "Good morning doctor, how are you today?, we are just doing our morning rounds, so we thought we would pop in and see you and check that everything is ok."

He replies, "Well thank you gentlemen, I am very well." The captain looks around the sickbay and says, "Well I am very impressed the sickbay is so clean and everything put away in its right place. A lot of ships that I have been a captain on, where the sickbay is the last place I would want to be in."

"Thank you captain for your kind remarks , but I cannot take all the credit, mytrainee nurse Sarah has that part all under control." The captain looks over at Sarah working away sewing up the white sheet around the body of the sailor that had died getting him ready for his burial at sea. She can see the captain looking her way, she lifts her head and looks at him. The captain nods his head at her.

She smiles back and nods her head as a sign of respect, then carries on with what she is doing.
The captain then tells the doctor, "we will be pulling into a port in a few days time, Is there anything you might need to top up your stores." He replies, "no we are all good thank you oh and by the way captain I have logged the sailor's death in my log book for the records." "Well done doctor, any way we must carry on with our inspections around the ship." Once the captain and the first officer had left the sickbay the doctor walked over to where Sarah was standing and gave her a kiss on the side of her face , she asks, "well, what's that for." He replies, "that's just to prove that I love you." They both start to laugh.

The months go rolling by at sea. Peter has taught Sarah a lot of his medical knowledge as the patients came and went through the sickbay. When they were quiet Sarah would read medical books that the doctor had lent her.

Then that big day came, There was a sound of excitement everywhere after they heard someone call out, "LAND AHOY, ITS THE HARBOUR OF AUSTRALIA." A big raw of excitement was being shouted out by everyone above on the top deck.

CHAPTER 6

WE HAVE REACHED AUSTRALIA,

WILL THIS CHANGE SARAH'S LIFE FOR EVER.

Sarah walks across the sickbay to where Peter is standing, she looks very worried and somewhat sad. He looks back at her and can see by her face that something Is wrong. "What's wrong?" He asks her. " Well we both knew this day had to come so what happens to me now . I suppose I'll have to go back into the prison system , that will mean I won't see you anymore." Sarah cries out, Peter replies, "I have been thinking about that myself. So what I am going to do is ask the captain and the first officer if they will write me out a reference on your behalf saying what a good nurse you have become. I will also write one out myself on how important it is for you to stay with me as my assistant and continue to work with me in the hospital, hopefully that will work.

    In fact Sarah I'll go and see them right away before things start to get hectic." Sarah smiles at him as he walks out of the sickbay. One hour goes by and Peter returns with a smile on his face. "Well that worked out ok. Both the captain and the First officer of the marines have written you very good references, so with my reference. I hope that will convince the Governor of the prison to let you stay with me and both work together in the hospital. At least we will be together each day until we figure out how we make our relationship legal.
    She replies, " I do hope so, I will be heartbroken if I am taken away from you."His head drops and looks sad . He

lifts his head and tells Sarah, "Come on young lady let us be positive about this, I am sure it will be ok."

A few days later all the women prisoners were ready to be taken off the ship and transported to a prison where they must carry out their sentences. Peter followed by Sarah walked up the wooden steps leading to the top deck. All the guards line the deck so no prisoners could escape even though they were chained to each other. Down the wooden gang plank the prisoner's walk until they reach solid ground which was something they hadn't done for months and months.

The women prisoners stand in line one by one. An officer stood in front of them. The Governor of the prison was also present. He stood there in all his glory with his medals pinned to his chest. Every one could see he was the big cheese and the main man in charge.

The officer had a clipboard with all the prisoners names upon it. The officer called out their names and as they answered they climbed onto a horse drawn wagon that would transport them to the prison.

Doctor Peter walked with Sarah down the gang plank , they stood there waiting to see if her name was called out.When the officer got to the end of his list he called over to the Governor, "Sir we are one short" The Governor came walking over and took the clipboard, he ran his finger down the list. "Ah yes I see a Sarah Wright." The Governor called out, "Whereis Sarah Wright did she pass away on the journey over?". The doctor stepped forward, he introduced himself to the Governor. "Good morning Governor, I am the doctor of the ship that brought the prisoners over from England." They shook hands. Doctor Peter asks the Governor, "please may I explain to you about the missing prisoner on your list? He replies, "please do doctor". "Well this woman that's standing next to me is Sarah Wright and she has been working with me as my nurse. I have personally trained her to a high standard and would like very much to take her with me to the hospital as a nurse and assistant."

The Governor looked at the doctor with a stern look, "Well " the Governor replies "I am afraid sir that is totally impossible, I have my orders from England and all prisoners must be firstly settled into the prison and put to work."

"Yes I know what you're saying Governor but she will be a great asset to me and our hospital, and I have three hand written references written by the captain, the first officer and by me, all telling you how good Sarah Wright is and how hard she works. In my opinion sir it will be a total waist of a nurse to be just stuck in a prison probably just stuck scrubbing floors."

The Governor tells the doctor, "ok, i will take your three references and read them when I get time, but just for now she is an ordinary prisoner just like the rest of them and I will not discuss the matter any further."

The prisoner Governor calls over to Sarah Wright, You must get into the wagon with the rest of the prisoners". Prisoner Wright climbs into the wagon with the other prisoners, "you will be going to prison like the rest of them." the Governor tells her.

Sarah glances at the doctor then drops her head as she does not want to show the feelings she has for the doctor as the Governor is still watching both of them closely.

She climbs up onto the back of the wagon and is chained to another prisoner. The back of the wagon is locked and pulls away with the doctor looking on.

The captain of the ship walks up to the doctor and say's, "I know it seems hard Doctor but he has his orders just like the rest of us. Tomorrow I have to go to the jail to get some papers signed by the Governor, I'll have a private word with him regarding your nurse as I can see the sense of her working with you in the hospital. It would be a shame to waste the nine months of intense training you have given her."He agrees with the captain and thanks him.

The captain did as he promised by speaking to the prison Governor the very next day. But all the Governor would say was, " I hear what you are saying captain but it is my responsibility to make sure that everhing runs smoothly and everyone is accountable. Firstly I must assess this prisoners behavior, remember she is a prisoner and not a nurse in our eyes. Maybe once she has proven herself and beenassessed correctly we can think about the situation again. Until then there's nothing to discuss, I am sorry but that's how the system works in this prison.

One month had passed and Sarah was in the prison work partat the laundry, hand washing uniforms, sheets and anything else that came into thelaundry on a day today basis.

One evening all the women prisoners were queueing up for their evening food when a women started screaming out loud in pain then fell to the floor holding her tummy. "Help, help, me someone please help me I am having a baby, the bloody thing seems to be stuck." The women gather around her not knowing what to do for the best. Some guards came running over but just stood there watching for a moment then they went to pick her up. Sarah called out," gently with her, the baby is probably in breach. Lets walk her very slowly back to that cell that's just behind you and lay her gently on the bunk." She tells another guard, "go fetch me some hot soapy water in a clean bucket and some clean towelling." Sarah walks into the cell where the woman is lying on the bunk. Sarah stands at the foot of the bed and tells the women " please open your legs as wide as you can so I can see what's going on.Sarah lift's up the woman's clothing where she can see her vagina. The woman is still screaming out loud. The guard came running back to the cell with the bucket of hot soapy water and some towelling and placed them beside her. Sarah puts her hands into the water, making them very soapy, then placed her right hand into the woman's vagina, the soap helps her hand move around. She feels for the unborn babies feet and pushes them upward twisting the babys body so the head was in the right place to be born. She tells the women to start breathing deep, in a fast fashion. Sahara can hear someone at the cell door, she turns and looks, It was the Governor standing there, She turns her head back to her patient telling her to push hard. As she does the baby is born alive and well.

Sarah washes the babies face and body that was covered in blood. Sarah gave the babies bottom a smack and the baby started to scream out loud. The Governor started clapping his hands a few times. "Well done", he tells her, "you have done a very good job. Remind me are you the women that worked with the doctor on the way over from England." "Yes sir." She replies. They both turn around and Doctor Peter was standing there. He asks "what's happened here, did you bring this baby into the world?" "Yes," Sarah replied. The baby was breach so I put my hand inside her and turned the baby the right way, all you have to do now doctor is cut the cord and check them both over".

Doctor Peter asked her, "where on earth did you lean to do that?" Sarah told him "well doctor I used to watch my mum. Lots of local people that had no money and couldn't afford a doctor came to our house for help. She helped hundreds of women in child birth, some were breach so I sort of knew what to do."

"Well done, you have probably saved two lives today, the woman and her baby."The Governor spoke up. "Yes, I watched and she was amazing. She didn't panic at all looks like you trained her very well."

The Governor approached the doctor. "Doctor please come and see me in the morning, maybe she might have more to offer than washing clothes in the laundry " the doctor thanked him. "I will be in to see you tomorrow morning sir, please forgive me Governor I must finish up on the baby and the mother."

"That's fine, now everyone back to your cells, guards get them back into their cells as quick as you can and no talking ladies"

The next morning the doctor arrived at the prison, he asked to speak to the Governor and was shown to his office. He knocked on the Governor's door, the Governor called out in a loud tone " please open the door and come in " Peter did just that, the Governor was sitting at his desk "please come in and sit down." The doctor looked around the office and observed lots of certificates on the walls.There were commendations for his prison work in England he congratulated the Governor on his hard dedicated work and for his certificates that were on the wall that proved it.

"Thank you," he replies "Now the reason I wanted to speak to you this morning is that I have re thought my earlier decision regarding your nurse. I have read the references that you gave me when you first arrived in this country and I can see that they stack up."

"After experiencing first hand how your nurse performed very well I am going to take a chance and release her into your custody. But if she breaks the rules in anyway she will be shipped back to this prison straight away and it will go down on your record that she was under your supervision. Now do you understand me doctor because I also have a reputation to keep up."

Doctor Peter puts out his hand, "thank you Governor, i understand everything that you have told me."

"Ok," says the Governor, "I have prepared a document for you to sign to say you take full responsibility for the prisoner. What's the prisoner name." He replies, "it's Sarah Wright." The Governor filled out the paper work and the doctor counter signed it.

The Governor shakes Doctor Peter's hand and tells him," I'll get a guard to bring her to you at the hospital a little later." The doctor thanks the Governor they once again shake hands. The doctor then leaves the Governor's office and walks slowly back to the hospital. He couldn't show any emotion on his his face but inside he was full of glee.

Sarah had no idea what was happening, two guards walked into the laundry and called out her name. Everyone one in the laundry stared at Sarah, all thinking to themselves what she been up to on the quite. Sarah looked at the two guards then stood up. One of the guards called out "Prisoner Wright come with us," she walked out of the laundry with them and back to her cell her head hug low as she didn't know what she had done wrong.

As she arrived at her cell Governor SPIKESLEY was standing outside of the cell She frowned at him. Sarah spoke in a very gentle way, "sir what have I done wrong." He looked at Sarah, well I am pleased to say Wright you haven't done anything wrong . As you know I witnessed your brave work to save that prisoner and her babyyesterday.So I asked Doctor KINGSWOOD over to my office this morning to discuss your future. As you know, you are a prisoner and you were sent here to Australia to serve out your sentence. In the rules it doesn't say where you have to work. I think you might be better off in the hospital as you seem to have those skills where you can help others. I have discussed this in full with the doctor and he has agreed to sign an agreement where he will take full responsibility for you. Let me tell you, "if you misbehave or try to escape or leave the hospital grounds, unless you have the agreement with your doctor, then I will make sure you go back to prison and serve the rest of your sentences under lock and key. Do you understand stand that?"

Sarah looks at the Governor with a stern face then replies, "yes sir I do understand totally, I promise I will not let you or the doctor down, especially as the Doctor has spoken up for me personally ".The Governor waved his finger at her, remember Miss Wright, I have been doing this job a long time. What it has taught me is not to trust anyone but now and again I have to trust someone. So don't let me down."Sarah thanked the Governor and again she told him , "I won't let you down sir." You can go back to your cell now and wait I will send a guard to take you from the prison over to the hospital The Doctor will have to sign some more forms then you are officially released from this prison and into the custody of Doctor Peter KINGSWOOD .

CHAPTER SEVEN

SARAHS DREAM OF WORKING IN HOSPITAL COMES TRUE.

Doctor Peter is sitting at his office desk in the hospital when he hears a loud knock at his office door. He calls out , "The door is open please come in."The door opens and standing there is a prison guards with Sarah, one of her hands was handcuffed by a chain on to the guards other hand. In the guards other hand were some papers for the doctor to sign. The guard speaks . "Sir, I was told to bring this woman prisoner over and hand her over to you personally .I was also told that you must sign the papers for her transfer to the hospital and I must take them directly back to the Governor's offices."Peter lent forwards and took the paper work read them and signed them.
The guard pulled out a key and undid the hand cuffs. Sarah rubbed the skin on her wrist as the cuffs where tight and made her wrist sore. The guard saluted to the doctor then left the doctors office closing the door behind him. Sarah and the doctor looked at one another for a few seconds.

Then Peter walked slowly around the desk towards Sarah, took one step nearer to Sarah their arms opened wide as they embrace each other, holdingone another so tightly it was like they were glued to each other. Their eyes meet for a few seconds then kissed one another with so much passion. They had missed one another so much but the love was still as strong as ever.

Peter tells Sarah, "darling I've missed you so much, I used to think about you every day and what it must be like in that prison. She smiles at Peter and tells him how on the long boring nights in her cell she would just think about him or what he might be upto, Were you reading a book or working in the hospital, that would see me through till I fell asleep and the next thing I would know is the guard knocking on the door to wake us all up."

"I was in some ways lucky because they had put me in a cell with Maria and Claire, the women I was friendly with on the prison ship coming over even though it was only for a few days or so. And I must say even though they were two hard nuts they both looked after me like I was there little sister. I hope one day I can pay them back for their kindness."

Doctor Peter tells Sarah about the hospital staff that work there. "I know you will like working in the hospital. The people here are really nice. We have a head nurse called Linda WADESTON and a couple of young women that come every day to help out.

We have a really nice man who used to be a tribes man and lived in what they call the bush, in other words to us, the out back.

In this country they call his type ABORIGINAL, which I think means someone who was originally from Australia. He is such a nice kind man that would do anything to help anyone. His name is George.I have also met his wife , her name is BOO she is also Aboriginal, they were married in a Christian church and the vicar over the years has taught them both to speak English."

"Right Sarah I'll take you along to meet LINDA WADESTON but don't worry I have told her all about you, some of your past and how I trained you as a nurse on the ship coming over to Australia."

Out of the doctor's office they go everything seems strange to Sarah she has never been in a hospital before especially in a different country in fact she had never been outside the EastEend of London before .

All the buildings were made of wood from roof to floor with small windows that lifted up to open and allow fresh air into the wards . There were ten beds each side of the ward and a large desk in the middle of the room where a nurse would sit doing her paper work and keeping an eye on the patient's. This ward was the men's ward. At the end was a double door that lead through to the woman's ward which was just the same as the men's, ten beds each side, and a few small rooms at the end .

Peter looks across the men's ward and sees nurse Linda looking at a patients arm. They both walk over to where she is standing, she turns around and smiles, "Doctor Peter speaks to her, "good afternoon nurse this is Sarah Wright, she is the young woman I told you about that came over on the ship with me and worked in the sick bay as my trainee nurse and now she is coming to work here in our hospital."

"That's very good doctor", Linda replied, "we could certainly do with some help.There are times when I don't know if I am coming or going." All three start laughing.Peter asked her, "could you please sort out a uniform for Miss Wright and would you take her under your wing for a while and show her where everything is in our hospital. I just know once she has settled in she will be just fine. Now ladies I must leave you both as I have my rounds to go on , I'll see you a bit later Miss Wright. maybe now we should call you nurse Wright." The doctor left them both and went on his hospital rounds .

Nurse Linda, tells Sarah "follow me and we will get you sorted out with a nice uniform."She followed Linda down the ward through the door at the end and into a store room.There she saw a large rack of uniforms, another cupboard was full top to bottom of bandages, Another cupboard full of pills and drugs . Also there was a large table full of medical instruments. Sarah could not stop looking at them, she was truly amazed at everything she could see.

Sarah choose a uniform that fitted her and tried it on, nurse Linda tells her, OK, that's a good fit you might as well keep it on especially as you're a part of the team now .

They walk back to the men's ward, " let's start at the first bed ,if you look at the end of the bed you will see the notes for this patient and on those notes you will see his name, his address and his contacts, like wife and children, we do that with everypatient whether it's a minor thing they are in for or something serious. That way we know who to contact should we need too, we also write what's wrong with them what medications if any they are on and as much information about the patient as possible, that way everybody knows what's going on with the patient."

Sarah looks at the notes and read's them , "yes, I see, what a good idea. Oh and I see you sign your name so other people can see who has filled the notes in." "Yes, That's right Sarah, well done for spotting that."

They walk from bed to bed reading every patient's notes so Sarah could see why the patients where in hospital, once they had finished in the men's ward they went through the door to the women's ward.

A large man with a dark complexion came walking towards them. Linda called out, "George, Please come and meet our new member of staff." George put out his hand so he could shake Sarah's hand , she responded and they shook hands .

Linda told George, "this is nurse Sarah, she has come over from England, she is not familiar with how we work in our hospital here in Australia , so if she ever needs any help please come and rescue her. They all started to laugh. George tells Sarah in a deep Australian accent, "please miss you can ask me for help and I will if I can"Sarah replies, "thank you George and if I can ever help you please ask." He nods his head and thanks her. "I must get on ladies, I have some deliveries coming into the hospital and I must attend to them." Off he walks, Out of the door of the hospital.

Nurse Linda asks Sarah, "have you been shown where you will be sleeping or your room?" "No nobody's told me anything about that Linda, we have been so busy walking and talking,I forgot to ask.""That fine come with me I'll show you your room, It's only small but it's private and it's your own space if you understand what I mean.""Yes I do know what you mean, sometimes it's nice to get away from it all and just be on your own."Linda agrees , "yes you are so right, hospitals are a lovely place to work but sometimes they can be a sad place too." Sarah frown's at her comment not knowing what might come in the future. They walked along the building where there were some small rooms. Linda opened a door to a small bedroom. ""Here you are Sarah this can be your room , There's fresh bedding in acupboard over there, so make up your bed as you like it . I need to get back to the ward now so I see you in the morning at 7.30. If you listen you can hear the church bells ring out the time on the hour, now you get yourself settled in and I'll see you in the morning. Oh and please don't worry about a thing, it will take a while before you remember where everything thing is , it takes time "

Sarah thanked her for her words of encouragement. As Linda left the room , she walked over to the large wooden cupboard and opened the door, smiled to herself as she held the bedding up to her nose and could tell they where brand new.

It made her feel extremely happy as she had never had new sheets before in her life. Not even when she lived at home in the east end of London with her dear old mum and her brother Robert.

Sarah made up her bed then decided to try it out. Her head lay snuggled into the cushion, she then stretched her body out across the bed and lay back with her arms tucked nicely by her side.

O my god she thought to herself , what a difference between this bed and the bed in the prison, which had a mattress made of straw. When the the straw moved or went flat you had to get up and shake the mattress back into position or just lay there all night felling very uncomfortable .

As she lay there on her bed her eyes started to become heavy and she drifted into a deep sleep and a deep dream started.She was back in the east end of London, back in her bedroom, Sarah was laying on one bed ,Robert laying on his bed , they where both laughing to each other, bothtelling each other funny stories, then mum came into their bedroom with some hot toast that she had made over the fire. Mum walks across the bedroom and kisses them on the side of their faces. Suddenly there's a loud knock on the door which wakes her up. She sits upright, wipes her eyes and calls out "YES who's there." A voice answers back, "it's me Sarah, it's Peter." Sarah jumps up from her bed and opens the door and there stands Peter with the biggest grin on his face. Peter asks well, "darling aren't you going to invite me in."

Sarah started laughing, "how did you know I was here." "I bumped into nurse Lindawho had given you a tour around the hospital and showed you to your quarters, sohere I am just checking to see that you have settled in ok."

He shut the door behind himself as he walked into the room, walked up to Sarah, put his arms around her and shyly kissed her on the side of her face. She looked into his eyes and put her loving arms around his neck pulling his head closer to her lips.This time it was a kiss of passion. They held one another so tightly that they could not be prised apart . Slowly they slid onto the bed still gripping one another tightly as if they where one.

Sarah cried out, "Peter I have missed you so much that I felt I couldn't go another day without being with you." " I felt exactly the same about you, every day every minute, you were on my mind even though I tried keeping myself very busy in the hospital, somethings would just remind me of you."

Slowly they undress each other and make love in a most passionate way.

CHAPTER EIGHT

SARAH STARTS WORK IN THE HOSPITAL

The next morning Sarah wakes nice and early she is full of excitement with the prospect of starting her new job in the hospital. She looks over to the side of the bed where Peter had been laying but had now left as he did not want to compromise their position .

The church bell struck six a.m. Sarah stretched her arms out even though it was Early the warm AUSTRALIAN suns rays where coming through the window..She walked across the room opened the curtains as wide as she could to let in as much sunlight as possible. She could already feel the heat from the sun that was beaming into her bedroom.

She washed, put on her new uniform. How smart she felt, her mother and brother would be so proud of her, she thought to herself . Once again the church bells struck out its chimes, it was now seven o'clock only thirty minutes to go.

Sarah walked back to the window and looked out she could see some gum tree's in the distance. Beyond that she could see the prison walls where she had spent so many restless nights.

She raises her head and looks into the sky ," good morning Mum, good morning Robert, Well I start my new job today at the hospital. I have met the most amazing man who is a doctor and I love him so very much and the good thing is I know he loves me in return and it is funny because it's a different kind of love to loving my family."

I promise you both that whatever it takes I will become a good nurse and one day hopefully younger people will look up and see my love and kindness that I give out to everyone. It was you Mum that instilled that love in to me". A few tears begin to trickle down her cheek Sarah takes a big sigh, then wipes away her tears from her cheeks Sarah leaves her room very excited for the day which lay ahead of her.

She walks though the hospital to meet nurse Linda in the men's ward. All though Sarah was early Nurse Linda was already there sitting at her desk in the men's ward reading some patients notes. She looks up at Sarah and gives her a wonderful welcoming smile, "well good morning nurse Sarah how are you today. Sarah replies, "I am very well thank thank you." "And thank you nurse Linda.? what for nurse Sarah " Oh for that wonderful welcoming smile you just gave me."Linda just laughed. glancing at Sarah and tells her. "Well I must say how smart you look in your new uniform." "Oh, that's so kind of you." Sarah replies. Linda stands up. "Right Sarah, today as it's your first day in this hospital Ithink it would be a good idea if you watch me and we will work together. That way I can show you exactly how we do things here." Plus why we do it in that fashion

Sarah agreed, "thank you," Sarah added, " i think that would be a brilliant idea."
They both walk down to bed number one. Nurse Linda started by taking the paper work that was attached to the rear of the patients bed. "I showed you yesterday briefly

about the patient's notes and how we write them up after each visit, now please read them carefully. You can see by these notes that this patient broke the upper part of his leg and also the bottom part of his leg. We have put him in splints and are keeping him in for now so he rests and does not try to put any weight on the leg." This man is a farmer and most farmers are terrible at doing what they are told to do. If he tries to put weight on his leg to quickly he could damage his leg so badly he may not walk on that leg again, so by keeping him in hospital we can stop him from doing that. Sarah replies," I totally understand." Sarah reads the notes.

"Yes, I can read what's been done." "That's very good," says Sarah.

Nurse Linda says to the patient, "good morning Mr. Smith, how are you feeling this morning." He replies, "ok thank you nurses but please call me Richard. They both Sarah and Linda answer at the same time, which make both of them start to laugh. "OK Richard." Sarah asks him, "do you need anything?" " A drink of water would be nice." He tell's her.

Sarah pours the water into a glass and hands it to him. Linda then tells Sarah to "pick up Mr Smiths notes again then write down the time that we spoke to Mr Smith, the time that we have examined him, the mood that he is in, that he is not in any pain   And put down he has had a glass of water. All this information could be helpful to a doctor should there be a problem". Sarah writes up Mr Smith's notes then clips them onto the back of his bed.

"Ok, that's bed number one done, on to bed number two."The first couple of hours just flew past. Sarah was by now feeling very hungry and looked pale in her face. Linda asks Sarah, "are you ok sweetheart." Sarah looks up and tell's Linda, " I am feeling a little faint, I haven't eaten since yesterday."

"Ok don't worry, come with me I'll take you to our lovely little canteen, I am ready to eat myself."

Off they wandered along another corridor of the hospital, they could smell fresh bread that had been baked that morning. Sarah's eyes popped open wide when she opened the door to the canteen and saw a wonderful range of food that was on offer.

There were all types of fresh fruit, eggs, pork, lamb, and of course a nice of pot tea.

She had never seen so much food in one place at one time, in her life. Standing there was porter George, he was filling up plates and putting them on to a trolley that was on wheels ready to take them to the patients that where in bed and could not get about. They looked over to George the porter , he looked up and smiled at both of them, Nurse Linda waved back, then called out to him,"Good morning Mr George, are you and your wife well," he replied, "yes thanks, we are keeping well and thank you for asking. George was speaking in his dialectof mixed Australian and English. " Good morning to you ladies, what a lovely day."

Linda replies, " I haven't seen much of yet " , all three start to laugh, porter George tells both nurses I must get on or my patients food will get cold. George walks off pushing his trolley in the direction of the men's ward.They walked along in front of the food, there plates in hand, filling them with any food they fancied but not wanting to look greedy at the same time.

Once their plates where full they found a nice seat next to the window where they sat down and started tucking into the food.The minutes flew past when Sarah got a tap on the shoulder. She turned her head slowly thinking to herself, I wonder who that could be, to her surprise saw it was Doctor Peter. Remembering what Dr Peter had told her that in public she must always address him as Sir or doctor Sarah decides to stand up and put her hand out to welcome the doctor, "good morning doctor, how are you." She asks . "Yes I am fine thanks , I see that nurse Linda is looking after you."

Sarah replies, "Oh yes sir she is looking after me very well." He turns to Linda, "thank you for showing her the ropes, I hope to see you both at some point during the day on the wards."

They smile at the doctor, Sarah is being very careful not to show any signs of emotion towards the doctor, he also cannot show any emotion back to her for the time being they must keep their love for one another a secret.

A year rolls by. Sarah is working very hard in the hospital. She has learnt so much and can even assist Doctor Peter in operations . All is going well for them and their love and devotion for each other is still as strong as ever.

Peter tells Sarah that he would like to buy a house that he has seen not far from the hospital. He tells her it is a big house with ten bedrooms and it's already to move into. And Sarah, I want you to give me your blessing on this house as one day it will be our family home.

"Oh Peter, of course you have my blessing but may I ask can you afford it as I have no knowledge regarding money or property,""Yes I can afford it, my brother and I were left quite a lot of money by our grand parents after they passed away , so the answer is yes I can afford to buy the house and still have some money left to furnish it with."

"My god Peter, did you say ten bedrooms." He started to laugh, "well Sarah we don't know how many children we might have."She gives Peter a gentle punch on the arm and says, "ten kids, did you say ten kids, I'll for ever be washing nappy's out. I think more like four if you are lucky."Both of them start to laugh.

CHAPTER NINE

TROUBLE ON THE WARD

All was going well in the men's ward that morning ,Doctor Peter was showing the Governor of New South Wales around the hospital on one of his monthly tours. Linda and Sarah where changing a patient's bandages on the other side of the same ward.

The door to the men's ward opened and a guard from the prison walked in chained to a prisoner. The guard told the prisoner to sit down on a wooden chair, which he did.
Nurse Linda looked over and called out to them, "please give me five minutes and I will be over to see you."
The prisoner officer call back, "thank you nurse." Around ten minutes had past and no one had seen them. The prisoner jumped off his seat and pulled so hard on his chain that it pulled the guard onto the floor hitting his head hard and knocking him unconscious.
The prisoner was screaming out loud like a mad man possessed. It was like he had the strength of two men. Everyone was now looking at the prisoner and wondering what was going on.

Doctor Peter walked over to where the prisoner was standing and tried to calm the man down. The prisoner then reached out and grabbed the doctor around his throat and starts to throttle him.
The nurses start to scream at the prisoner to stop. Peter's legs fail him and he drops to the floor but still the prisoner is holding on. Sarah runs across the ward and

jumps on the prisoner's back and bites his ear that hard a piece of it came off.

She starts screaming at the prisoner you bastard leave my Peter alone.

The prisoner grabs his ear blood is streaming down the side of his face. Peter rolls away from the prisoner and gets to his feet, two more guards come running into the ward and hold the prisoner tightly on the floor. The guard that brought him in is also up on his feet and they grab the prisoner off by his feet to a side ward. Sarah looks at Peter and run at him she throws her arms around, Sarah face is ashen white, she is trembling with fear and temper. Peter still feeling disorientated responds and puts his arms around Sarah. Nowthey have both shown their affection for each other to all those on the ward including Peter Foster the Governor of New South Wales and nurse Linda.

Sarah and Peter separate , Peter dusting himself down from being on the floor whilst Sarah straightens up her uniform.

"My god Sarah, if you hadn't acted as quickly as you did I think I would have been killed.

The doctor looks down on the floor and saw a bit of flesh, walks over and picks it up. He looks puzzled then realises it is a piece of someone's ear, he quickly lifts his hands to his head and checks on his own ears. They are both intact. Thank god, he thinks to himself.

Peter looks at Sarah and frowns at her. "She tells Peter It was the only way I couldget him off you. It was an old trick the men used in the east end if they had a fight with a sailor or may be someone they didn't know." "To be honest Peter I don't know what came over me. As you know I am not a fighting person but I just could not bare to watch that horrible man hurt you."Well done Sarah , he certainly was a man possessed." Nurse Linda and the Governor came over two them both. The Governor told nurse Sarah.

"My god you are a very brave woman nurse Wright, very brave indeed, I only hope you're around if I ever get into trouble."

Nurse Linda put her arm around Sarah's shoulder as she could see she was still in shock from the whole incident. Big George the porter came bursting through the doors, "I have just heard about the trouble in here is there anything I can do?""Yes there is something you can do, bring us a large pot of Tea to calm our nerves."

George replies, "yes sir, I'll go right now, please give me say ten minutes and I will bring you all back a nice hot fresh pot of tea." Off he went back through the door of the ward . Once they had all drank their tea Linda and Sarah decided to carry on their duties looking after the patient's in their care. Governor Foster and doctor Peter carried on with their monthly inspection of the hospital.

Once they were on there own, the Governor told Peter "she's a good woman, verystrong in character, she will make someone a good wife one day."

The doctor smiled at the Governor, "sir I know I shouldn't say this so please don't tell me off, I would like to be the man who marries her one day."I know that technically she is still a prisoner in Englands eyes but I can also see she cares for you very much.I think I will write a letter to England and tell them how she jumped in and saved your life with no thought of her own .I will recommend for her courageous actions & that she gets a full pardon, that way if they grant it you will be able to get married when you want" Peter puts out his hand and they shake hands vigorously.

The Governor told Peter , "ok Peter stop shaking my hand so tight it fills like my hand is in a clamp and thank you for thanking me, but let's hear back from England first."The Governor also told doctor Peter, " do not mention this to anyone not even Sarah, let's just keep this between ourselves."

"Well all I can say Governor, is if Sarah does get a pardon I'll be the happiest man in Australia."

The Governor smiles, "well doctor let me tell you I am more than happy with the way you are running the hospital . Doctor I have a meeting in government house later so I had better be on my way. I think there's a ship going to London that leaves tomorrow so I want to get that special letter written to the parole board and on it's way, the quicker the letter gets there the better, I promise I will recommend her for a pardon."Once again Doctor Peter thanks the Governor.

CHAPTER TEN

WHAT A FABULOUS HOUSE

Doctor Peter thought long and hard about the letter that the Governor was sending to England regarding Sarah's parole and decided not to say anything to her as Governor Foster suggested, also he didn't want Sarah to be so disappointed and very upset if the parole board did not grant it, so he just carried on with his life as if nothing had happened.

The next day Peter went off to view the house that he had seen up for sale. The bonus he thought was that the house was only a few minutes walk from the hospital.

Peter meet the agent selling the house directly outside the man pulled out a large bunch of keys and opened the front door , once open they both went inside to have a good look around and make sure it was the sort of house peter was looking for. Peter and the man walked up the staircase that led to the bedrooms Peter asked the agent, "just how many bedrooms does it have." The man confirmed that the house had ten bedrooms. Peter asked the agent is that not unusual for a house in this area to have so many bedrooms." The estate agent. replied, "well sir the man that owns the house had a very big family ." Both men started to laugh.

They came down the stairs into the passageway over to the right was a large kitchen/dining room full of cupboards, floor to ceiling. There was a large range type cooker, a large sink with two draining boards each side of the sink, the other end of the room was a massive farm type table where lots of people could sit around and eat. Across the hall was a lovely big sitting room with a big open range fire place. Peter thought to his self what a great big room for all the family or friends to sit and relax in. Next to the sitting room was a large bathroom with a cooker that was used for boiling the water so they could have a nice hot bath, or it could be used for washing the clothes. The house was just perfect. The doctor thought to himself.

Peter asked the man, "can we now look at the outside of the house." They walked through a large wooden door which was half glass so you could see right into the garden .Plus the glass door let the wonderful sun light into the room.

It was a large garden, mainly grass, a few swings, a metal children's slide, and in the corner of the garden was a large wooden shed. Peter just stood there and scratched- his head in amazement. The man who had owned this house before had just thought of every thing.

Both men walked back inside the house. Peter told the agent "I know the asking price and I am very happy to pay the asking price for the house as it is, it's just perfect , plus it's only a five minute walk from this house to the hospital."

The agent smiled at Peter, "well you can't do better than that sir." You're offering the asking price. The agent also asked Peter "may I ask you sir what is your work at the hospital," "well sir I am the doctor there." Plus I run the day to day working off the hospital, it is totally my responsibility to make the place run smoothly.

The estate agent replied, "That's very good sir I know where to come now if I ever get sick."

Peter replies, "you do that young man you do that." Then Peter tells the man, "I would like to show my friend the house and get their opinion. "That will be fine Sir, "replied the estate agent. Peter tells him " I come back tomorrow with my friend and after that I will give you my answer about the purchase of the house."

The agent tells Peter "yes that's fine, I will see you here tomorrow, shall we say the same time as today." "yes, OK " Peter replies, but if I get stuck or there's a emergency i will let you know somehow. Peter tells the agent, " please don't sell this house to anyone else. before you get my answer."

"Sir, you have my word I will not sell the house until you say yes or no by tomorrow evening."Doctor Peter walked back to the hospital, his mind was jumping all over the place, thehouse was perfect in every way. He walks into the ward where Sarah was working with Linda and called over to them , " Linda may I talk to Sarah for a few minutes please.""Yes of course Doctor."Sarah walked over to Peter with a frown on her face, "what's wrong doctor," Peter replies with a big grin on his face "nothing at all Sarah, I have been and seen the house that I heard was for sale. I had a good look around it and I think it's is just perfect for us so I have made arrangements for us to view the property tomorrow and if you like the house I will buy it."

Sarah touches Peter's hand very discretely then whispers to him, "That's just why I love you Peter you always think of me first."

He gives her a gentle loving smile in return, then calls over to Linda, "have you got a minute please Linda ," "yes of course, how can I help you?" Peter walks across the ward to where Linda is standing. He tells her, "by now you know that Sarah and l are quite fond of each other. Tomorrow I want to show her a property that I am thinking of buying. It's only five minutes from the hospital so could you cope on your own for say around hour, but if there is an emergency we will not go.

Linda says, "of course she can, bless her, I hope you both like the house, Doctor Peter""Thanks nurse Linda." He also tells her. "I will just pop over to tell her that I have had a word with you and you have given your blessing."

That night came and went so fast .After the morning rounds were over and everything was tidy in the wards and Doctor Peter had finished his rounds, written out his report for the day, he walked back to the men's ward to find Sarah just finishing her paperwork.

He walked over to where Linda standing talking to a patient . He asked nurse Linda, "is it still ok for me to take nurse Sarah from the ward. Hopefully it will only be an hour or so before she is back,"Nurse Linda replies with a big happy smile , "off course it is, we will all be fine, now off you go."

Peter nods at Sarah, "Ok let's go", they walk out of the ward and made their way to the house where he was shown around yesterday. The estate agent was waiting for them.

The doctor introduced Sarah to the salesman. The man puts out his hand and they shake.

" A very good afternoon to you madam, please step inside." As he opened the front door.

He asked them, "would you like me to show you around the house or would you like to walk around on your own." " We would like to take our time and walk around on ourown, thank you" Peter replies.

Peter took Sarah's hand and they started to climb the staircase to the bedrooms.

In and out of the rooms they walked. The rooms all had nice high ceilings, bigwindows with beautiful curtains that had been left by the previous owner, also built in wardrobes and large fireplaces, just in case it got a little cold in the wintertime.

Peter could see Sarah was getting very excited. Well he asked, what do you think so far?"

She just looked at him, she couldn't speak, then she just burst into tears, he put his arms around her and gave her a great big hug. Sarah tried hard to console herself.

"Oh Peter it's perfect, I can imagine children being very happy here as they run around playing." "Well" he replies, "so far so good let's go down stairs and I'll show you the other rooms."

She wipes her eyes they walk back down the grand wooden staircase to the ground floor. The sales man is standing in the sun shine in the garden, he looks through the open door at them , he smiles and asks, "what did you think of the bedrooms." Sarah replies, "they are just wonderful."

Peter then shows Sarah the large bathroom."look Sarah they have thought of everything, see they have installed an extra cooker so you can boil up hot water for a bath or for washing the cloths or whatever you want to wash."

She replies "that's just brilliant."

"Ok now I'll show you the kitchen/dining room." They walk along the hall that leads to the kitchen, Peter opens the kitchen door and Sarah's eyes open as wide as they can go.

She is amazed by the size of the kitchen/dining room. She runs over to the cupboardsand starts opening all the doors ",just look Peter, at all the wonderful cupboards, there's so many of them , this kitchen is just amazing, oh and look at that big range cooker. My dear old mum would have just love it in here".

Peter just started to laugh, he could see that Sarah was excited and she felt very happy in this house. He thought back to when he was growing up, how he was so lucky to have a loving family that cared for one another, just how happy and safe he felt in their family home.

Sarah walked back into the hall, "what's in this door?" Peter opened the door, "darling have a look." She pushed the beautiful carved wooden door open to see in front of her a very large lounge room with a big open fire place , four sets of windows that looked out to the front garden. The windows still had beautiful handmade curtains that went from the top of the window to the floor. She turned around, ran over to where Peter was standing and jumped into his arms. They both laughed loudly as he swung her around the room.

"So do you think you like the house." Sarah replies with a big grin on her face, like it Peter, i just love it I think it's like a palace where a princess would live." Well my little Sarah, you'remy princess and I love you very much."

"Oh Peter, I do love you, you're just so kind to me." They embraced and kissed.

"Right Sarah, let me show you the back garden," "yes, yes' she replies, "i can't wait."

They walk out into the back garden. Once again her eyes open wide at the size of the back garden.

"Look, there's a slide for the children, some swings and there's also a large wooden shed.

Peter this place is just amazing." Peter asks, "so shall I buy it then." Sarah says in a most excited way. "Yes yes and yes again."

Peter calls the salesman over who was standing the other side off the garden and puts out his hand as the salesman gets closer.

"Well sir it looks like we are buying this house." The estate agent smiles at them and says, "i can just see that you two really like it here and there is going to be a lot of love and happiness in this house. "Doctor KINGSWOOD can you come over tomorrow to our office, we can start the paperwork and get you moved in as quickly as possible."

As they shook hands, Peter told the him, "if nothing goes wrong in the hospital tomorrow, I'llbe over to your office some time tomorrow . My bank is in Sydney so it will be easy for me to organise a deposit." The estate agent thanked Peter then told him , "I'll see you tomorrow sir." Peter then turned to Sarah and told her " I think we had better walk back to the hospital and get back to work." As they left the house and walked to the hospital Sarah kept looking back at the house in total amazement.

A few weeks had passed when the salesman walked into the hospital and asked the woman on the reception please, "may I speak with Doctor Peter KINGSWOOD." She told the man "please wait here sir, I'll see if he is available and what is your name." He replied "myname is Nicholas Taylor, he knows who I am."

The receptionist walked off to find the doctor who was is in his office and brings him to thefront of the hospital where Nicholas Taylor is standing. Doctor Peter looks surprised see him standing there. Nicholas puts out his hand to the doctor, "good morning doctor and what a lovely day it is."The doctor agrees with him, "yes it is a very nice day." Nicholas hands the doctor a large padded envelope.

He takes hold of the envelope but looks a little surprised, "are there more papers to sign?"

"No." Nicholas Taylor tells him, "here are the deeds to your new house and inside theenvelope are the keys to your house, it's all done and dusted now you are the proud owner of your very own house in Sydney."

Peter raises his hand to him and they both shake hands.

He thanks Nicholas for all his help in organising a quick sale and making it all run smoothly.

He tells him, "well sir you know where I am if I can ever help you or assist in anything else."
Peter walks along the corridor off the hospital to find Sarah on the ladies Ward. Sarah looks up at him and says, "is everything okay Doctor.""Yes nurse Sarah, in fact everything is very well , when you get a few minutes will you pop down to my office as I would like to have a word with you." Sarah smiles at him, " ok that's fine please give me, say fifteen minutes and I will come down to your office."

Once Sarah's work was completed she walks along the corridor and arrives at Peter's office. She knocks on the door, Peter calls out, "come in Sarah."

She asks, "is everything okay." He smiles and replies, "yes my darling, everything is fine and you see that brown envelope on my desk, that's the deeds and keys to our new home in Sydney. "

Sarah runs to Peter and throws her arms around his shoulders, "thats wonderful news."

She tells him. "I never knew that these things could be done so quickly." He replies, "I know,To be honest Sarah

I didn't know how it could be done so quickly myself, anyway it's all done it's our home now."

CHAPTER ELEVEN

THREE MONTHS GOES BY

That three months after buying the house in Sydney the time just flew past. The doctor had employed two builders to work on the house most days. Theywanted every room in the house washed from the ceiling to the floor, then repainted in nice bright colours. Once a room was finished they would go to a nearby store and choose the furniture for it. The house was coming together brilliantly. Even though Sarah did not have any experience in furnishings and colours she just seemed to have a natural flare for it. She remembered what her mum had told once, "keep a room bright, keep a room light."

It wouldn't be long before they could move in, even though Peter would have to inform Governor SPIKESLEY and get his permission for Sarah to stay at the doctor's house at night, that was the rules and Peter was not about to break them.

One day a letter was sent to the hospital addressed to nurse Wright. The receptionist took the letter along to her as she was working in the ladies ward.

She walked over, handed the letter to Sarah who almost froze as she looked at the letter. She could see by the embossed stamp on the envelope it had been sent from the prison.

The receptionist asked Sarah, "are you ok, you have gone white, do you want me to get you a chair or call some one?" Sarah just hung on to a bed and asked the receptionist, "please would you ask nurse Linda to come here." The receptionist rushed off to the men's ward and found nurse Linda.

"Nurse Linda," the receptionist called out , "I think nurse Sarah is having a funny turn, shehas asked could you come to the ladies ward."

Linda thanked the receptionist and rushed along to the ladies ward where Sarah was standing holding on to a bed looking in a pretty bad way, very white in the face and faint.

She asks her, "what's on earth wrong Sarah, she replies, "look Linda, i have been sent this letter from the prison and I am too frightened to open it. I bet they want me to go back to serve the rest of my sentence behind bars. I could accept that, but I haven't done anything wrong. I would miss you and my Peter so much and think I would just pine to death."

Linda tells her, "come on, let's go to a side room, we will open the letter and see what this letter is all about."

They walked along to a side room which is only a few minutes away. Once they were inside Linda tells Sarah, "Sarah just try to relax and sit on the bed, I'll open the letter and let's just see what's this all about "

Linda opened the envelope slowly then pulled out the white paper letter and read it. Sarah asks , "please put me out off my misery. They want me back in prison don't they."

Nurse Linda starts to read the letter "It just say's that Sarah Wright prisoner of his majestythe King of England must report back to the prison in Sydney tomorrow at ten am. You must report to Governor SPIKESLEY, bring this letter with you and show the letter at reception, thats all it says."

Sarah burst in to tears, " I knew it , just when things in my life start to look ok and I feel happy things go wrong for me." It's the story of my life.

Linda asks Sarah , " will Doctor Peter go with you just in case there's a problem. "I could ask him but I don't want him to worry, he's got the house to think of and the worry of the hospital, so no I won't ask him." Nurse Linda shout's at Sarah, "don't be so silly Sarah "You must tell him, he will be devastated if you were taken away from him, I just know how much he loves you. I can just see it in his eyes when he looks at you. So promise me you will talk it over with him before you go over to the prison." "Yes if you think I should." Sarah tells her Linda. "I think we should go back to the ward now in case there's a problem." Sarah tells Linda.

A few hours pass and Doctor Peter walks in to the men's ward where the nurses were changing the sheets on a bed. He walks over to speak to a patient, Linda looks at Sarah and tells her "you had better show him that letter or I will," Sarah nods her head and agrees , "ok, I will as soon as he is free."

Doctor Peter walks over to the nurses and asks, "how's everything nurses," but he can see from Sarah's face that something was wrong. Linda prompt's her, "come on you had better tell him." Doctor Peter looks at Sarah and asks. "Tell me what, what's going on, have you done something wrong." "No doctor it's nothing like that, Sarah tells the doctor. " I have had a letter from the prison and I must report there tomorrow at tenam. I have to report to the Governor of the prison." Sarah starts to panic, "do you think the Governor is going to put me back in prison." Sarah tells Peter as you know I haven't done anything wrong so why me.

Peter just looked at Sarah and told her , "don't worry, I'll come with you, If there's a problem I can speak up for you." " Oh please, come with me Peter I'll be ever so grateful , " it's fine Sarah, try not to worry too much, i am sure it will be ok."

Sarah lies on her bed all night, although Peter has told her not to worry she can't stop, thethought of her not seeing Peter every day would drive her out of her mind. She thought,I have been taken away from my dear mum , they have taken my beautiful little brother away, my life would be finished without Linda and my Peter. Slowly

Sarah fallsinto a deep sleep. The next thing she hears are the church bells ringing. She lays on her bed and counts the bells. It's six o'clock, I must get up now and get ready for work then off to the prison by ten o'clock. No she thinks, I'll get there for around nine thirty, I must not be late.

Sarah had a full wash and put on her nurses uniform. She then rushed off to work on the men's wards as she did every day. I I need to know that all my patients are ok, washed and fed before I go back to the prison. Every time she thought about the prison her tummy flipped over. Now stop this, she thought to herself, what will be will be. I suppose this time tomorrow I'll be working back in the laundry room again.

Those few hours that morning just flew past. Sarah tried so hard to put on a brave face for all her patient's. Doctor Peter came onto the ward extra early that morning to do his rounds. He also wanted to be all prepared when he took Sarah back to see the Governor in the prison.

Peter could see that poor Sarah was very upset and worried about this so called meeting. So he thought to himself I must stay quiet in case I say the wrong thing and it makes her cry. When it came to nine thirty, Peter and Linda walked over to Sarah. Peter spoke first, "shall we make our way over to the prison and get all this nonsense sorted out." Linda try's to reassure Sarah by saying, "try not to worry and I'll see you later", they embrace.

Peter and Sarah walk over to the prison. It's a very hot day in Sydney and theywere feeling the heat of the day, even though it was just coming up to ten o'clock.

Peter was holding the letter in his hand. He knocked on the prison door and a small window opened. The guard that stood behind the thick wooden door spoke, "yes how can I help you." Peter showed the guard the letter and he opened the main door that lead into the prison.

By now poor Sarah was shaking and felt quite faint. The guard took them into a room where another guard was present, Peter showed him the letter. The guard read it and said. "Follow me sir, I'll take you to the Governor's office, which he did.

Once there, the guard knocked on the Governor's office door, he called out, "Come in, Peter opened the door they walked into the Governor's office.

Please sit down the he told them. Peter sat down but Sarah told the Governor that she would prefer to stand.

"I am surprised to see you here doctor as my letter was addressed to Miss Wright," Peter says, " you know Sarah and I are good friends so I wanted to see what this meeting was all about and maybe help advise her should she need it."

Sarah could not take it anymore her poor nerves had just about had enough so she spoke out to the Governor herself. "What have I done wrong sir, I worked as hard as I could in the hospital, I just can't think what I have done. Please don't make me go back into prison sir. Whatever I have done wrong I am so sorry for, please just let me live out my sentence working in the hospital where I am helping people."

Peter looked at Sarah surprised, he had never seen Sarah speak out to any body before.

The Governor walked around from his desk and held Sarah's hand for a moment, "please just sit down and let me explain to you ok."

Sarah nodded her head and the Governor had her sit next to Peter.

"Right you two let me explain what has happened, if you remember around six months ago we had a prisoner jump on to the doctor and was trying to strangle him to death, you Sarah, came to the doctor's rescue. Without any fear for your own life you jumped on to the prisoner's back and wrestled him to the floor. I was there and witnessed your bravery my self and without your bravery that day the doctor would have lost his life."

"Any way Miss Wright, I wrote a strong letter to the parole board back in England. I think about six months ago, Recommending you for parole for your bravery, plus I told them about your work in our hospital.

The parole board have written back to me and have approved it .In fact they have decided to give you a full pardon, your sentences is now squashed, you are totally free to do with your life as you wish."

Nurse Sarah head fell into her hands and she started to sob heartily, tears drops were falling onto the floor. Peter jumped up from his seat and put his arms around Sarah Peter told the Governor that Sarah's crying was half in relief and half in happiness.

The Governor spoke out to them. "Most people that I given this news to just laugh out loud, may even scream, but never cry."

Peter and Sarah walked over to where the Governor is standing and shake him by the hand , Doctor Peter asks the Governor, "sir does this mean that Sarah can stay at my house that I have brought in Sydney and maybe one day we can get married."

He replies, "yes Doctor, she is a free woman to do as she pleases."

They walked away from the prison arm in arm, proud and in love.

"Please Peter, can we first give nurse Linda the good news as I know she is also worried about me. "Yes of course we must." He replied.

They walked into the ward where Linda was sitting at her desk filling out a report about a patient. "Well tell me," she asked," how did you get on, I can see they didn't keep you in so that must be a good thing."

Can I tell her Sarah says, "yes I think you should," Peter replies, "well Linda you're not going to believe it, I have got a full pardon on my sentence I am the same as you, a free women to come and go whenever I please."

Linda asks why what's happened. Sarah says ,"well do you remember the prisoner that was brought into the ward and then went mad and tried to strangle Peter and almost succeeded until I jumped on his back and bit off his ear to make him let go of Peter's throat."

"Yes, "replies Linda, Well the Governor wrote a letter to the parole board back in England and told them if it wasn't for my brave actions the poor doctor would have died.

So they wrote back and gave me a full pardon .What do you think about that.

Linda jumped up from her chair and threw her arms around Sarah's neck, "oh that's wonderful news, just wonderful." Sarah says "I hope you don't mind, I haven't eaten since I read that letter so if it's ok with you Linda can Peter and I go to have something to eat in the canteen, then I will be back to work I'll work like a beaver."

Linda just smiled at Sarah, "that's fine my darling, you two enjoy your lunch.

Off they went, down the ward and into the canteen.

CHAPTER TWELVE

O MY GOD NOT TYPHOID

Sarah is going from patient to patient to check they are all ok, when the doors burst open and a man is pushed in on a trolley by George the hospital porter. Doctor Peter rushes in behind them.

Nurse Sarah call's out to the doctor, "what's wrong." Peter call's back I am sure this man is suffering from Typhoid fever. We need to put him in a room on his own to isolate him just incase."

"Ok Doctor, I'll get a room ready." Says George the porter as he pushes the trolley through some doors at the end of the ward and into a empty room. The porter helps the man off the trolley and onto a bed. He was in a bad way and sweating profusely, being sick at the same time.

Doctor Peter calls over to nurse Linda, "nurse quickly get me some cold water and some Clean cloth so we can wash him down and try to bring his temperature down." "George please can you open the windows wide, grabs those scissors and cut of all his clothing off, Take them outside and burn the lot." The porter does as he is asked.

The doctor ask the man how are you feeling, he replies, "I feel terrible sir. I have a bad Thumping headache, my muscles ache and I can't stop being sick."

The doctor then checks him over and he can see a small rash all over his body.

Peter also asks "tell me have you had any diarrhoea.?" The man replies "yes doctor, all the Time. I think my wife might be coming down with it also. What do you think it might beDoctor?" Peter replies "It has all the signs of Typhoid Fever." He asks the doctor "Typhoid Fever, what the hell is that."

Peter looks very worried but tells him in a calm manner, "its a fever that is caused by bad sanitation or contaminated water." He looks at the doctor and frowns.

"Doctor could you send someone around to my house and check out my wife and our kids, please . " Doctor Peter tells the man, "yes, don't worry, I'll get someone to go around to see them this afternoon." The man thanks the doctor.

Doctor Peter takes George the hospital porter to one side and tells him. "pick up all that man's clothing, including his shoes and burn them, take yourself to the washroom, strip off your hospital clothing, wash yourself thoroughly in vinegar, That will kill any germs.Make sure all your hospital clothing is also burnt.

And nurse Sarah keep washing him down from head to foot, we must get this man's temperature down or we will lose him."

"Nurse Sarah, after you have finished looking after him, you must then get yourself off to the bathroom, get bathed, wash your hands and face etc in vinegar. Make sure your clothes are put in a sack ready to be burnt." Nurse Sarah looked at doctor Peter almost in disbelief as she had never seen Peter before in semi panic mode.

Nurse Sarah asks the doctor, "what is this illness called." He replies, "It's called Typhoid Fever and if we don't get to the root of it and find the cause of where it's coming from it can spread like wild fire, Sarah it could kill hundreds may be thousands of people if we can't stop it. So Sarah listen to me please, keep washing your hands with soap and water and don't touch your face especially your lips mouth, don't eat anything without washing your hands and poor neat vinegar on your hands the vinegar will act as an antiseptic."

Sarah asks the doctors ,"do they know how it starts or what causes it."Well Sarah, some doctor's were studying it in England and they all came to the same conclusion, bad sanitation.By the way I think we will have to try and make up some masks and figure out a way to keep our uniforms clean. Maybe boil them in hot soapy water that includes vinegar. I think I must now get myself washed and then get to my office so as I can read up on this Typhoid fever and see what is the best way to try and deal with it before it deals with us."

He stay's up most of the night reading and making plenty of notes along the way.

Peter comes out of his office and looks for George the porter, when he finds him he tells the porter to take this letter over to the prison for the attention of Governor SPIKESLEY.

Peter tells George,"tell him to read the letter straight away then come over to the hospital as I need to talk to him very urgently."George takes the letter and off he goes.

Peter then walks along the wards and to the room where the poor man had been put yesterday who was suffering with the Typhoid fever. He found the man body, with a large white sheet that had been place over him, the man had passed away in the night.

Peter lifted the sheet and peered at the man's face and body, by now his body was cold as ice. The doctor touch the mans head it felt like marble ,the doctor put the sheet back over the man and walked out of the room to find Sarah. It was now a round six in the morning .Peter thought Sarah would be sleeping and did not want to disturb her so Peter decided to go back to his office and wait and see her a little later .Plus hopefully the Governor from the prison will come over to the hospital. So I can explain what I think is happening. Peter was reading his medical book about Typhoid when he could not keep his eyes open wide any more, the doctor rested his head on the table then fell fast asleep.

After a couple of hours he gets woken up by a loud knock on the door, the doctor jumps to his feet in a total daze , he then walks over to his office door and opens it. Standing there were two men , one he knew.

It was the Governor from the prison, Joseph Spikesley, the other man was the Governor of New South Wales, a man call Peter Foster.

He invited them into his office. Governor Foster introduces himself, "I was planning on coming over to the hospital at some point to meet you, but I have been extremely busy. So when I saw Governor Spikesley early this morning he told me you had sent him a letter telling him we have a problem and you needed to see him. I thought I would come with the him to see what was going on and if there was anything I could do.

He asks them to sit down and tells them, "Gentleman we have a very bad problem on our hands ," both the Governor's looked at one another then Foster ask's, "problem what kind of problem may I ask." The doctor carries on speaking, "i think we have a possible outbreak of Typhoid fever about to hit us."

Governor Foster ask's in a harsh tone, "Typhoid Fever, How can that be possible."Governor Spikesley sits quietly because he knows just how serious Typhoid can be as he has seen an outbreak of it in London when he worked there many years ago.

Governor Foster ask's the doctor, "I have heard of Typhoid Fever but what actually is it,what causes the fever and just how bad can it get."

"It is caused by bad sanitation, normally it's raw sewage that gets into the clean water and contaminates it. People just don't know that the water is bad for them. Firstly governor or governors should I say, we must find the source of the problem. If we don't it will be a majorproblem for the health and well-being of all that live in New South Wales and I must warnyou tens or even hundreds of people could lose their lives if we don't get it under control."

The Governor goes on to ask the doctor what evidence has that it's typhoid.The doctor tells governor Foster, " a man was omitted into the hospital yesterday and his wife later that evening, subsequently both of them have died.

I examined their bodies and found the illnesses they had added up to only one thing, typhoid."

There is another knock at the office door, Doctor Peter standing up, "please excuse me gentlemen," he walks over and opens the door, standing there was nurse Sarah.

He invited her in to the office, he introduces her to both men, even though she had met Governor Spikesley before at the prison. Sarah began to speak to them.

"Sirs, in the last few hours we have admitted another eight or more people, five men and three women. They had the exact symptoms as the man and lady that were omitted to the hospital yesterday and died." Doctor Peter thanks Sarah for bringing that information to me .

Doctor Peter tells Sarah, "It's the same procedure as yesterday, ask the porter to get all their clothes, including their shoes, and burn ever thing. Make sure that all the staff are told to keep washing their hands and rinsing them in vinegar. That will help kill the germs and stop the staff getting sick"."Sarah can you also tell the canteen they must not wash any food in cold water , all water must be boiled first even when drinking and please tell the canteen that they must do this straight away as this is a very serious illness, i will be down to them to speak to them also. " Sarah nods to Peter then leaves Peter's office. Doctor Peter tells both Governor's I think what we will do is move the male patients that are already in the hospital in with the women patients that will give us one clear ward to put any one that comes in with the typhoid fever all together.

We might also have to put up massive canvas tents to house everyone with typhoid If it gets out of control that way we can keep the hospital separate for our normal ever day patients.I can't stress how dangerous Typhoid Fever can be. It could gentleman wipe out half of our population if we don't get it under control.

Doctor peter looks at both men and say's, "gentlemen we will need to pool all our resourcesto stop this typhoid in it tracks."

Governor Foster asks the doctor, "Doctor what can I do to help." He replies, "theproblem is sanitation. Firstly everyone must boil the water they drink. I can only assume that sewage is somehow getting into the clean water and contaminating it. If we don't get to the bottom of it and find the problem, and I know I am repeating myself but hundreds maybe thousands of people could die from it. All the hard work that has been put in to building this colony will be destroyed in one foul swoop."

Governor Foster ask's once again, "right doctor what is it you would like me to do first." He tells him, "first you have to divert the raw sewage away from any lakes or streams, Then dig new trenches to take it out to sea. Also dig new trenches from the lakes and streams so that the wells that people draw their water from is fresh and clean. Check all houses, works places and any social gatherings, that there is no contaminated water there.

Any bucket of water must be thrown away. Tell everyone, all water must be boiled before drinking or even washing in it. Everyone must be informed of what's going on and how dangerous the contaminated water can be.

But I have to warn you both we cannot sit on this, you must put every available man that you have, diverting and separating the water and every day you waste is more lives lost, Sir's do you understand me. Time is of the essence."

Governor Spikesley also asked the doctor, "what can I do to help. The doctor replies, "sir you must get ever spare male prisoner out under guard and help with the digging of the trenches. I need 40 women prisoners sent over to the hospital to help my staff. I will need every bed scrubbed and washed in hot water, walls floors and everything must be keptscrupulously clean. Then Gentlemen if we pray to god we might just win the war against this terrible illness."

The Governor's got to ther feet and shook the doctor's hand, "we will do everything in ourpower to combat this fever, whatever you need doctor, please just ask and we will get ithere." The doctor thanked both the men, he told "Governor Foster again the main thing is get hundreds of people out there and sort out the sanitation and get the trenches dug, You must get clean fresh water coming into the town and the bad sewage going in a complete different direction out to sea. These channels must be dug, say, half a mile from each other so one cannot affect the other and gentlemen think of the future, the way Sydney is growing you must think of the infrastructure needed in ten or may be twenty years down the road or we will probably have this problem again but then affecting millions of people."

Governor Foster tells the doctor, today we will rally the troops and tomorrow we will start digging"

Governor Spikesley also said, "I will sort out the people you need to help out in the hospital when I get back to the prison, tomorrow morning they will be on your door step bright and early. We can then erect the large tents plus spare beds and any equipment you might need."

The Doctor told Governor Spikesley, also Governor you must get all your prisoners to wash their hands in boiling hot water, no drinking water unless it's been boiled, tell your kitchen the same, the Governor replied, " I understand Doctor ".

Once again the doctor thanked both men, "I think we should meet every couple of days, lets say at midday here at my office for a progress report, from the trench digging and what's happening in the hospital to the staffing levels we might need." Both the Governor's left the doctor's office with a plan in their mind of what was needed to be done.

The very next day true to his word there were 40 or so women prisoner's waiting outside the hospital all ready to go to work and help out in any way they could.

Nurse Linda looks out of the hospital window and sees the women prisoner's waiting in the morning sun. Both Linda and Sarah go outside to greet them. Peter had already briefed them on what to say and how to train them on the work they had to do.

As the women prisoners were walking into the hospital after their briefing someone called out to Sarah, "It's us Maria and Claire ,"Sarah was so excited to see them she puts her arms around them and hugs them so tightly it almost felt like she was strangling them.. "How are you" she asks." "We are both ok but look at you in your nurse's uniform." "Yes I know, but I have learned so much, I'm not a bad nurse now even if I have to say so myself".

Maria asks, "so what's going on, all we know is there's some kind of fever going around andthey sent us over to help out." "Yes," Sarah explained "it's a thing called Typhoid fever and it's very dangerous. What we need is for everyone to help out in the hospital by cleaning the beds, washing down walls etc to help keep the hospital clean and fight infection.

So nurses and the rest of the staff can do the medical stuff." Sarah tells both Maria and Claire, "please ladies whatever you do , please keep washing your hands, do not put for any reason put your hands near your mouth and wash your hands before you eat." Claire says, "Christ is it as bad as that." Yes" Sarah replies, "it is very contagious so please be careful."

As the days went on both Governor's stuck to their word. Hundreds of troops and prisoners alike were out in force digging trenches wide and deep from the large lake of fresh water into Sydney .

More troops and prisoners were digging trenches from a large cesspit down to the sea at the furthest point away from Sydney. The work was so hard as everyone was working in the heat of the sun.. Many men would pass out with exhaustion and fatigue.

They even built large fires so they could have teams of men working through the night, as they knew they were battling against time.

In the hospital grounds prisoners built large tented areas where the typhoid cases could be kept separately from general patient's and other tented area's where the staff could bath or wash down.

A large pit was dug so all of the clothing from the typhoid victims could be burnt and the cloth used to wash and cool down the typhoid victims was also burnt.

After a week or so the whole of Sydney seemed to be in chaos. Lots of people took there families to live in the bush to try and escape the Typhoid fever that seemed to be breaking out every where.

The hospital was overrun with patient's and dead bodies were taken away to be burnt every day. Nurse Linda walked onto the ward to find Sarah, "when you get a minute can I have a word with you."Sarah raised her hand as a gesture that she heard her and she will be over in a minute. Sarah finished off what she was doing and walked over to where Linda is standing.

Linda asks asked her to follow her , which she did, to a large room in the hospital. She opens the doors and sitting there were around fifteen small children aged five to ten years of age, some crying for their mummy others in a total state of shock.

Sarah looked at Linda in dismay, "Who are all these children" she asked. She replied "these children are all orphans, their parents have died of typhoid and have no where to go. I have been getting them all fed and cleaned each day but now it's too much, Idon't know what to do with them".

Sarah walks over to them, she kneels down and puts her arms around as many as she can, If not all of them."You poor darlings," she told them. She looks up at Linda and asks, "why is there nowhere for them to go." "Well as this is a new country, I suppose that they have never had this problem before. There probably hasn't been the deaths of both parents or a relation has probably stepped in and taken the child.

But this is something unprecedented in Sydney." At that moment tears started rolling down Sarah's face, "my god" she says", "these poor children can't just go wandering around the streets. No one to feed them, no one to put them to bed at night and no one to guide and love them . That is so wrong, the poor little mites,"

She tells Linda,' "I have plenty of room in my house, so they can come home with me."

"But what will Peter say," asks Linda. "Well he will close his eyes and run his right hand through his hair,Think for a moment ,then I will know he will agree with me that it is the right thing to do." because he is also a very caring man." Both Linda and Sarah both give the children a great big hug. Sarah tells them, "don't worry children. You can come home with me and my husband , we will look after you all." Sarah asks Linda,"please can you go and organise some food for them, I will go and find George and ask him if he has any old beds for the children and if he has, get them taken up to Peter's house it's only five minutes away."

Linda goes off and organises some nice hot food whilst Sarah goes off to find George.

Sarah explains what's happened about the poor little children to George . George drops his head and Sarah could see a few tears rolling down his cheeks, the tear drops fall onto the ground. George quickly wipes his eyes and tells Sarah, "don't worry miss, I will get some of my friends to help me and I'll get some sheets, blankets , pillows." "Oh yes, that will be marvellous, thank you ."

Now that everything was getting organised, Sarah went back to work on the wards as they were so busy. Once she had caught up, Sarah walked outside to where the large tents were housing the patient's that had typhoid fever. Working away like a pair of beavers were Maria and

Claire, Sarah saw them and walked over to join them. "Hello Marie, Hello Claire , how are you both, I haven't seen you for a couple of day's."

The women looked up, when they saw it was Sarah it cheered them up straight way. They put their arms around Sarah and gave her a big hug.

Maria told Sarah, " It's so nice to see you are you keeping well." "Yes," She replied, "I'm not too bad. I had to make a quick decision earlier today which was quite an important one."

"Why, "asks Claire , "well it has turned out we now have some very young children that have lost their parents to this bloody typhoid, I have just found out that in Sydney, they are not set up for these problems, there's no work houses or orphanages where these poor little mites can go .I haven't told doctor Peter yet but I am going to take them all home with me. We have the space in Peter's home why not," Maria told Sarah, "God Sarah, that's is a fantastic thing to do, but what about the doctor, what if he say's no." She replies, "well ladies, that's a risk that I am prepared to take, I don't mean this in a horrible way but I wouldn't sleep at night not knowing where those poor little children were. Plus knowing the kind loving man Peter is, I am sure he would think the same as me."

Maria and Claire both spoke out my, "god, you're a very brave woman. That is a massive responsibility." Sarah replies, "to be honest I just feel I want to give these poor little children a chance in life. A chance that they never gave my young brother."

"Yes, that's true," Maria says.

"Any way, apart from that how are you girls getting on." " Yes not bad," Claire tells her, "It's much better than working in the prison laundry for 10 hours a day." "But it is so sad watching people die each day." Sarah agrees, "yes it is ."

"Right Girls" I think I'd better buck up the courage and go and find the doctor and tell him the good news." Sarah eyes rolled to the back of her head, Then sigh's. Both Maria and Claire smiled at her.and tell her, " good luck."Sarah walked through the wards looking for Peter, She sees Linda and asks, "haveyou seen doctor Peter on your travels." "Yes, last saw him about 15 minutes ago, he wasgoing to his office." She thanked her, then walked down the hospital corridor to his office. She knocked on the door, Peter called out, "please come in." She turned the door handle, walked into his office and sat in a chair opposite his large wooden desk.

"Well hello darling," Peter said, "what's wrong Sarah," he asks. "How do you know something I wrong. "He smiles, then ask's the question again. "What's wrong Sarah I can always tell when you have a problem because you always lift your right hand up to your hair and twiddle with it. So come on Sarah what's wrong."

Well Peter' I had to make a big decision which involves you and me but I didn't get your permission first and I now feel bad, not about what I have done but not speaking to you first. I am sure you will feel the same as me when I do tell you."

"Ok Sarah, you can tell me now, i am sure we will be able to sort it out between us.".

"Right, i will come straight to the point. There is in a room in the hospital with lots poor little children whose parents have died of Typhoid and now have no one or nowhere to go. I asked nurse Linda and she told me there are no work houses or orphanages for these poor little mites to go to". Peter looks hard and straight at Sarah. "So what are you proposing to me."

She says, "I think we should take the little mites home with us until we know what's happened to them." He looks into the air and stares at the ceiling giving him time to think about his decision that he is going to make regarding the children. I understand where you're coming from Sarah, But we have our jobs at the hospital and I don't know how we would have the time for such a commitment." She replies, "yes I do understand what you are saying Peter but I just cannot see these little children pushed from pillar to post , please can we just take them all home even if it's just for a little while."

He then asks Sarah, "where would they all sleep, we haven't got that amount of beds in Our house for them to sleep on."

"Oh Peter, I was sure you was going to say yes straight away, I told George to take the old beds that he had stored away to our house and set them up for the children. He has spoken to his wife and his friends which have come to the hospital to help take the beds around to our house and set them up along with some nice clean bedding that he had stored."

"Looks like you have already made up my mind for me Sarah", "Peter please don't say it like that, just walk with me and see the poor little soles sitting in a bare hospital room not knowing where they will be sleeping tonight or where there next meal might come from, It's so pitiful. It takes me back to when my mum was very ill and we had not eaten for days, that's what made me and Robert go out in desperation and do what we had to do just to survive. So I know what fear is."

They walked along the corridor's of the hospital to where the children were waiting in a room. Sarah opened the door and they both walked into the room. Peter took one look at the poor children just sitting there, some crying for their mothers, some in totalshock and fear for their lives.

"Oh yes Sarah, you have definitely made the right decision, I am so sorry I doubted you. You're right, we must do what we can for these children, we can take them home with us tonight and get them settled in. You can have a few days off and let's just see how it goes."

Sarah walks over to where the children are sitting on some wooden benches, Sarah kneels down so she was at the same level as the children, Sarah tells the children "please don't be frightened, my name is Sarah and this is doctor Peter we have room in our lovely house not far from here where you can all come and stay for awhile.I have to pop back home to see that you all have a nice warm beds to sleep in. As soon as I have sorted it out I will come back for all of you." Sarah also asked, "have you all eaten now." One little girl answered in a sad voice , " yes thank miss, nurse Linda brought us all some food .

CHAPTER THIRTEEN

THESE POOR LITTLE CHILDREN

Sarah walks back to their house where she finds a hive of activity. There are lots of aboriginal men there including George and his wife . George walks up to Sarah and tells her, "this is my wife Boo, she is very good at organisation and she has done a great job here today. She has told us men exactly where to put all the beds and she has made them all up with sheets and a blanket, so they are all ready for the children."

Sarah thanks Boo and kisses her on her cheek. Boo all though grateful for her kiss to the side of her face was slightly embarrassed by such actions because in Australia white people do not kiss or touch Aboriginals. Boo thought to herself this is a very kind and loving woman.

Boo and Sarah walked up the stairs to the bedrooms, Sarah looked inside each bedroom and was so pleased by all the hard work George, Boo, their friends had achieved.

They walked back down stairs to where everyone was standing. Sarah climbed on a chair and called out at the top of her voice, "excuse me everyone, I would like to say a big thank you all for all your hard work. As you know we have had a massive problem with the typhoid fever which has caused many deaths and it now appears we have some poor innocent children that have lost both parents to the typhoid so doctor Peter and myself are bringing all the children to our home here as I cannot bare the thought of them going here or there and nowhere to go."

Everyone in the room clapped at Sarah's speech, she was not expecting that, and was somewhat embarrassed by their actions because she had never given a speech before.

Sarah then asked George and Boo, "please would you come to the hospital with me and help bring the children back to the house as some are small and may need a hand."

Everyone in the room then offered to help, one saying,"if we all go we can all hold a child's hand or carry one back." Sarah replies by saying,"thank you all so much, you are so kind. Let's go, I think the quicker we get the children out of the hospital and back here the better it will be for them."

Off they went all walking together back to the hospital, along the way Sarah noticed people stopping and staring at the group of Aboriginal people all walking along together, that upset her quite a bit although she did not say anything to anyone, she knew there was a problem and at that point she just registered her thoughts in her mind.

Once they got to the hospital Sarah told everyone because of the typhoid fever out break they should all remain outside the hospital and just stand in the garden.

Only Sarah and George walked into the main hospital to collect the children. They walked along the corridor towards the room where the children were waiting.

As they opened the door Doctor Peter came walking along with nurse Linda, " well that was good timing,"yes" Sarah agreed, and told both them of the great progress that George, Boo, plus all their friends had achieved back at the house, And that the friends were waiting outside the hospital so they could help escort the children safely back to the house.

Peter shook George's hand and thanked him heartedly. Linda walked up to the children and started getting them ready, some had little coats to put on some just stood there in what they had . Peter tells Sarah, "well I am ready to come home now all's well at the hospital so we can all go together."

Sarah tells the children, "ok children, lets go." Some of the children were walking. The others Sarah, Peter, Linda, and George picked up and took them outside where George's Aboriginal friends where waiting to carry them back to the house.

Once back in Peter's house all the children sat on the floor in a line, Peter call's out to the children "Right children is anyone hungry. " All the children put their hands up quickly, "Ok , lets see what we can rustle up for you." Peter then turns to Boo and asks," Boo, please can you go into the bathroom and run a bath of nice warm soapy water, So once the children have eaten they can have a nice bath before bed."

George went off with Boo to help with the bathing, Peter went to the kitchen with Sarah to help make a nice plate of food for the children. Once the food was served up and all the children had been bathed both Sarah and Peter thanked George and Boos friends for all their fantastic helped with the children.

Sarah, Peter, Boo, and George carried the little mites up the stairs to their beds. They where all individually tucked up into their beds. They then kissed everyone on the side of the face and wishing them good night, some children replied other's just fell asleep as their heads hit the pillow. They crept down the stairs quickly as they did not want to wake up the little mites, they where all completely washed out. Boo asked Sarah, "tomorrow morning would you like me too come around nice and early and help you with the children as it will be far too much work for you on your own. Maybe be for the first few mornings it might be better for me to bring a few of my women friends too."

Sarah jump up from her seat, "oh yes please Boo, if you and a few friends could come that would be wonderful thank you very much." George and Boo left the house and walked home feeling happy in their hearts that they were helping in some way.

Peter asks Sarah, "Darling I hope you don't mind me asking, now we have the children here it's going to be a very large responsibility for you. I know you have done it for the right reasons but I don't want you to become unwell with the worry of it all."

She looks at him, "yes, i can understand what you are saying but someone has to step in and help out, I just believe life is a destiny like a ship setting off around the world never knowing what port it is going to stop at. Maybe this is my destiny to look after poor little children who have no one in their life to love them or care for them. As for looking after them maybe I might have to get help from Boo and her fiends along the way. Yes I know it will all work out Peter, just look how God bought you to me, the best man in the world."

Peter smiled at her, "you are such a lovely person Sarah, I think I am the lucky one."

Bright and early as promised Boo and a couple of woman friends turned up at the house all eager and ready to help. Boo knocks the door. Some white folk were walking past,They stopped and asked them why are you knocking at that door, a white person lives there.

Sarah opened the door and smiled at Boo and her friends.

"Welcome to all of you, please come in."Sarah looks at the white folk in the street,smiles and nods her head at them and says good morning. She shuts the door behind her. The white folk shrugged their heads and carry on walking .

Sarah called out to all off Boo's friend's, "thank you all so very much for coming to our home to help us with the children, It's very kind of you. Shall we start by going up stairs to where the children are in there bedrooms. Please take them down stairs to the bathroom, wash their hands and faces then get them dressed ready for their breakfast. Maybe we can play with them in the garden afterwards." "Yes, that's a good plan." Sarah tells herself.

All the woman walk slowly up the wooden staircase that leads to the bedrooms that the children are in. They walked from bedroom to bedroom saying, "good morning children, please get up now it will soon be breakfast time and I bet you are by now feeling hungry."

Most of the children were awake and ready to get up but some of the smaller ones were still asleep, so the women gave them a gentle tap on their shoulders to wake them.

Once all the children were up they slowly walked down the stairs one in front of the other until they got into the bathroom to wash their hands and faces and get dressed. Boo and Sarah at this stage went into the kitchen to get some food prepared.

All the children sat around a large table waiting for their food. When Sarah and Boo carried out a large plate of hot sausage with bread and butter all their little eyes popped wide open.

The food went down a treat with them all.
Peter went down stairs all ready to go to work at the hospital. He walked into the kitchen and kissed Sarah firmly on the the lips, most of the children just burst out laughing at the site of them kissing so early in the morning.

Peter picked up one off the sausages and ate it quickly before Sarah could see. "Right, you lot I am off to work." He then walked along behind the children and kissed them on the top of their head to show a sign of affection for each and every one of them.

"Goodbye everyone. I'll see you all later tonight."Sarah and Boo wave goodbye to Peter the children were all too busy eating their food to bother.

When they had finished eating, Sarah took them all out into the bright sunshine to play in the garden. Sarah told them to sit down on the grass so she could talk to them.

"Ok children let's start by asking you all your names." Sarah had a pencil and some paper so she could write them all down, also making a note of where they lived, their parents names and any more information that she could list down about that child.

Sarah thought that if she starts a file on each child that would go a long way in the future should a problem arise.

One by one Sarah wrote down enough information regarding every child , but some were so young that they only knew their first names and had no idea what their address was, but anyway Sarah thought at least that's a start. Boo came into the garden after washing up all the breakfast things . She asked Sarah, "I will stay here with you but is it ok for the other women to go now?"

Sarah said, "of course they can go , Boo would you look after the children for a moment while I thank them all." " Yes of course I will Miss Sarah."

Sarah stood up from sitting on the grass with the children and walked into the house where Boo's Aboriginal friends were standing, "thank you so very much everyone for your kind help."

The women smiled at her some understanding what she said and others explaining what she had said too them. She lent forward and kissed each one of them on the cheek.

Some of the aboriginal women went a little red in the face and some just burst out laughing, which pleased Sarah a lot. One of the women said to Sarah, "we will come again tomorrow to help you.""Oh yes please, I'll look forwards to seeing you again in the morning, thank you once again." Sarah shut the door and walked back into the house then out to the garden sat down with Boo and watched the children running around playing with each other. Sarah told Boo , just look at those children running around Boo, this time yesterday most of them looked half dead, it goes to show what a good night's sleep, some food and a little kindness can do. Boo nods to her in agreement, she told her my friends tell me that they all like you very much and think you are a very kind women. "Oh Boo, please thank them for that comment and tell them I like them also."

Peter walked home from the hospital that evening at a fast pace, he could not wait to get home and see Sarah and the children. He walked into the house and called out,"Sarah where are you darling."I am here Peter, in the dining room talking to Boo and George.please come and sit down with us." He smiles, "sure' is everything ok, are the children all ok." "Yes they are all fine and we have had a wonderful day with them. But it has been full on Boo and her friends have been amazing and are coming back in the morning to help again." He replies "well that's good Sarah, I have been worried I would get home and you would be stressed and upset."

"No I am fine Peter, but please can I talk to you in private." "Yes of course, let's go In to the kitchen." When they get there she throws her arms around his neck, hugs him tightly and tells him, " oh Peter I have missed you so much today." He hugs her back and tells her how much he loves her too. "Peter can I ask you a question without you being cross with me."

"Yes of course what's wrong?" "Peter, do you think we could employ Boo and one of her friends to help with the children?" Peter replies, "yes of course we can." Could we also get George and Boo to stay in one of the bedrooms upstairs then we have the proper set up here in the house. George will still work as your porter at the hospital, and Boo will be here at the house to help me with the children. Also once things sort themselves out I can still maybe work part time at the hospital if you need me." "Yes that fine Sarah, but please remember we can only fund this so far, let's not worry about that right now though."

Once again, nice and early, Boo's friends turn up to help with the children, this time it was just a little easier than the day before as they used the same routine as yesterday. Bathroom first, then into dinning room for breakfast and take the children into the garden for a good run around.

Sarah told Boo that she had discussed the situation with Peter regarding both her and George moving into the house. That way it would be a lot easier and safer to take care of thechildren. Boo agreed.

" Also Boo," Sarah asked, "could we employ one off your friends to work with us, help with the children, and maybe a few domestic jobs like make the beds and tidy up etc

"Ok," Boo tells Sarah, "there is a particular person that is very good, would just love to work here and she can speak English."

"Well that's brilliant," Sarah told her. She ask's Sarah, "what does brilliant mean I do not know that word , Sarah just laughed, "sorry Boo , brilliant means very good, I am happy with that decision."Boo just smiled at Sarah and nodded her head, "ok, I understand"

As the weeks passed by, things got better and a lot easier, mainly because they had developed a nice simple system of doing things. Boo and her friend worked very well together and the children were all settled in at the house.

Sarah said to Boo, " as everything is running ok would she mind if she went to the hospital a few days a week, just part time, as she missed nursing. Boo replied, " I thinkthat's a good idea, I can cope well with my friends on the days you are away."

So Sarah went back to the hospital for a couple of hours every few days to help out, especially as the typhoid fever was still active, although a little calmer as everyone was now boiling the water that they drunk.

Nurse Linda was working in the mens ward one afternoon when a guard from the prison brought in a hand cuffed prisoner to where they were working . The prisoner was covered from head to foot in blood, some his, and some from other prisoners that he had been fighting with.

Nurse Linda ran over to the prisoner. She told the guard, "put the man onto a spare bed.

She instructed the prisoner to lay down so she could access the his injuries . The guard asked Linda, "please Miss, would it be ok if I just cuff one hand to the bed because I really need to go to the toilet." Linda replied, "yes, that will be fine."

Sarah had finished what she was doing and came over to help with the patient. They started to cut away his prisoner uniform to see if he had been stabbed because there was so much blood .

The prisoner looked at Sarah and called out in a rough accent to her. "I know you from some were , let me think, O yes I remember you, you were the bitch on the ship that lied and said I tried to rape you."

Sarah went completely white with horror. The prisoner's hand that was not cuffed to the bed came up and grabbed poor Sarah around the throat, it's was so tight Sarah could not even call out. Without a second thought nurse Linda picked up a metal bowl full of water and threw it all over the prison. But this did nothing the prisoner he didn't even flinch. Linda then started hitting the prisoner over the head with the metal bowl, screaming out as loud as she could. But even this did not make the prisoner release poor Sarah from his clamp like grip and was by now semi unconscious and falling to her knees.

The ward doors burst open and in ran George who just grabbed the prisoner's arm and hand that was hanging on to Sarah's throat and pulled and pulled until he freed poor Sarah from his grip. The prisoner was screaming out loud like a lunatic that had gone completely mad.

The ward doors open again, this time it was the prison guard who pulled out his large black wooden truncheon and hit the prisoner across his chest which brought him to his senses.

They dragged him off the bed and out of the hospital.

Sarah sat down on a chair that Linda brought over. Linda asked, "what the hell was that all about," she held her throat as she was still in pain from the prisoner's grasp, Sarah tried to talk but nothing came out.

Nurse Linda went and got her a glass of water. The doors of the ward burst open and Doctor Peter rushed in. He looked at Sarah sitting in the chair "my god what's happened, I've just seen a guard and George dragging a prisoner out of the hospital."

Linda came back into the ward holding a glass of water and handed it to Sarah. She took the water and drank it in one foul swoop. Peter put his arms around her shoulders and gave her a massive hug. She just burst into tears and was sobbing uncontrollably.

After four or five minutes she consoled herself and stopped crying. She told them that he was the man on the boat who tried to rape her coming over from England and had beat her so much that she had to go into the ship's sickbay for treatment.

Peter and Linda just stood there in disbelief totally dumbfounded by the prisoner's actions. Sarah said, " he told them that I had lied about the attempted rape and it was all my fault that he was in prison" She carried on, "Peter you saw how bad he had beaten me and if it wasn't for the officer of the marines who came into the cell and saved me he probably would of had his way and raped me. "Yes. I remember that, it's how we met. You were in a very bad way. To be honest I thought you might have concussion he had punched you that hard."

He told her, " I think it might be a good idea if you go home and just rest. When George gets back I'll get him to walk with you. I'll make sure I am home early tonight as well."

Sarah just sat back in the chair, she agreed with Peter without an argument. George was soon back from the prison and walked Sarah back to the house.

Peter was doing his rounds later that day when nurse Linda stopped him and told him, "doctor we have another Orphaned child just sitting in reception crying, it's a little boy. He only had a mother and she passed away.

Peter said, , "when I finish my round I'll go to reception and take him back to our house with the other children."

Peter and the little lad walked home. As they walked home he told the little boy, "I know its hard losing your dear mother but you will not be alone, we are looking after other children that have lost their parents and they are all now very happy living with me and nurse Sarah,"

The little boy stopped crying and cheered up only a little. Peter opened the door to his house and as soon it was open they could hear all the children laughing and playing. Sarah looked over to Peter and saw a young lad standing there Sarah being her went straight over to him and asked, "what's your name."

My name is "Joseph Miss" Sarah lent down and put both arms around him. "My name is Sarah Joseph, and this is Peter. He is the doctor at the hospital and if you don't have any other family you can stay with us and we will look after you." The little boy then threw his arms around her and buried his head into Sarah's shoulder. Peter asked the boy, "have you eaten today." "No sir." He calls out to Boo, asks her to take Joseph into the kitchen and sort out some hot food for young lad.

A little later they looked over and saw him playing with the other children which made them feel very happy.

CHAPTER FOURTEEN

THE TWO GOVERNORS COME TO THE HOSPITAL FOR A MEETING WITH THE DOCTOR

A few weeks pass by. Peter was sitting in his office, very busy doing his paperwork when there is a knock on the his door. He stands up from his desk, walks to the door and opens it. There was Governor's Foster and Spikesley. "Come in and sit down. Doctor Peter tells them, welcome gentlemen and thank you both for coming over to the hospital andhow may I help you." Governor Foster answer's "we thought we would come over to the hospital to see you and talk to you about the typhoid".

The doctor tells them. "I think we are over the worst of it, we are not getting so many cases in the hospital and fewer people are dying from the fever. I think most people are boiling their water before they drink it, that's helping the problem no end. But as I have told you before, we must get to-the bottom of the problem with the sanitation and that's the only way it will ever be sorted out for good."

Governor Spikesley replied , "I have had every male prisoner and a lot of our guardsworking on this for over a month now and we have completed our work on the project.The main sewage from the town now runs completely out of the town and in to the sea miles way.The fresh water runs from a separate trench no where near the sewage, into the town. The gates for the fresh water will be opened tomorrow. But we were wondering is that enough. would it be a good idea if everyone in town boils there water forever? Even though the water is fresh from the lake."

Peter replies, "Gentlemen yes, yes, yes that is a great idea. I think that would be a good way forward and maybe the answer to the problem."

Doctor Peter tells them "it may be a good idea to make it a new law." Governor Foster then asks him, "I understand that you have under taken to take in all the children that have lost their parents." "Yes sir that is correct, but I must point out that it was Sarah's idea and I think it was because she is such a kind loving person. As you know my job is running the hospital, Sarah with the help of two other women look after the children I must point out these two women are Aboriginal women, kind and hard working."

Both Governor say that they have no problem with them being Aboriginal and that they are both very pleased with Sarah's efforts at what she is achieving for the community.

Doctor Peter then tells both the Governor's, "Sir's' while we are on the point about looking after and raising the orphaned children. I fund this completely on my own from some money that my family left me, but I won't be able to fund it forever."

Governor Foster replies, "well you probably don't know but we have our Town Council meeting each month, the next one is due in ten days time so why don't you come along and we can put it to the council to help you fund it . I can't promise anything as we are always short of funds." He thanks Governor Foster for his information and asks him, "please sir, could you put this matter on the agenda." "Yes Doctor I will do that with pleasure." The Governor's stand up and shake Peter's hand, "before we go are there any more matter that we need to discuss", doctor Peter tells them both "you should congratulate yourselves on the speed that you started the work on the sanitation and what a fantastic job you have done getting the work completed in a remarkably quick time. Between you, you have saved hundreds may be thousands of lives." Both Governor's thanked Doctor Peter for his kind word's. Governor Foster then thanked the doctor for all his help in advising them on how to tackle the typhoid outbreak and how they both look forward to seeing him at the council's meeting in ten days time. They then left Peter's office.

When Peter got home from the hospital that evening he told Sarah about the conversation that he had with the Governor's. He told Sarah about how all the sewage trenches had been dug and were transferred a different way out to sea. How new freshwater trenches had been dug from the lake directly to the town and it is now going to be law that everyone has to boil their water before drinking it."Peter also told Sarah "that he had mentioned to the Governor's that his personal funds were going down as he was funding out of his own pocket looking after all the orphans."

Sarah was so pleased with the fact that it would put an end to the typhoid and stop people from dying. But it might take a few more weeks before it all settled down. He also told herabout the meeting with the council where they might be able to apply for funds to help look after the orphans as his own money was starting to run low. She asked Peter,"why did you not tell me about the fact we were running a little low on money. "Sarah we only have about six months money left in the bank and one day it will run out. A lot can happen in six months so let's cross that bridge if and when we get to it." She looked worried.

A few days past and Sarah walked into the hospital when Linda came up to her, Sarah asked Linda,"what's wrong?, I can tell by the expression on your face some things not right." "Well Sarah, it's your friend from the prison, Maria, she's not feeling very well, she was washing down one of the typhoid patients when the man became sick. She tried to help him but he started to vomit and some of it went over poor Maria's face.

Although she washed herself she is starting to feel unwell".   Sarah asked,"when did this happen," "yesterday,"linda replied, "but Maria didn't tell anyone." "Where is she now?" Sarah said ,"we have put her in a side ward."

Sarah rushed down to the side ward, as she opened the door and Saw poor Maria she could tell straight away Maria was not well. Her face was ashen and she looked completely washed out. As she walked up to Maria , Maria shouted at her. "Stop, stay away, I don't want you to catch whatever I've got and it's more than likely this bloody typhoid fever shit. I washed down some poor man who had it. When he vomited it went all over me including my face so now I think that I have it."Sarah tried to relax Maria by telling her "Look Maria, some people pull through, not every one dies from it." ""Listen Sarah, I have always had bad luck, so if anyone will croak from it I will."

Sarah calls out to Maria "look darling I will go and find doctor Peter straight away, he will tell us what to do and to make you better." Maria smiles at Sarah but in Sarah's heart she knows that the typhoid fever will see her off.

Sarah walked all over the hospital to find Doctor Peter. Eventually she found him and asked "Please could you come with me and see my friend Maria, she has, I think contracted the typhoid fever. She is a prisoner that has been working and helping the typhoid victims. A man vomited all over her whilst she was washing him down , some of the vomit went on her face." "That's not good Linda."Peter replied. "Where is she? " Shetold him that Linda had put her in a side ward. They rushed down there, walked in and found poor Maria in a coma.

Peter opened the large window to try to cool the room down a little but the heat of the day was quite intense.

Linda asked doctor Peter, "is there anything we can do for her," "just keep her cool, to try to break the fever." "I am afraid Sarah it's in Gods hands now." "Please Peter would you mind if I stay here and nurse her, she has been a good friend to me and always watched my back."

"Off course you can but please be careful yourself, keep washing her down with cold water to try and bring her temperature down. If she wakes up try to be careful I don't want you catching it." "I will, "Sarah tells him. Oh by the way Peter would you find her best friend Claire Marchant, she is working still in the outside tent helping the typhoid patient."

He smiles, "ok Sarah , I'll go and find her and I'll send her over, that way she can help her as well." "Thanks Peter, I know she will be very happy to do that."

Sarah goes off and gets a bucket of cold water and plenty of clean cloth so she can start the process of washing down Maria to try to keep her cool and break her fever.

She hears a loud knock at the door and calls out, "please come in." The door opens and in walks Claire Marchant. "Oh God," Claire calls out then puts her hand over her eyes as she is totally shocked to see how poor Maria is so bad.

"I knew that she didn't feel that well but I didn't realise it was this bad." Sarah told Claire, "she got the typhoid fever, I have spoken to doctor Peter and he has told me the only thing we can do is try to keep her cold and bring down her fever." Claire asked, "what can I do to help?"

She said "I think a good idea might be if I wash her down in cold water you pick up that cotton sheet that's over there on that chair, tear it up into say two foot by two foot squares and try to fan her with it, that might just do the trick."

Claire does just exactly what Sarah has told her. Sarah would every ten minutes or so feel Maria's body to see if it was cooling down which it seemed to be.

After about one hour of both girls working very hard to try and get their friends temperaturedown Maria's eyes open up wide. They move to the left and right, looking at both of them, "Where am I, what's happening to me, I feel very strange." she says. "You're unwell Maria, you got a bit of a fever, but don't worry Sarah and I will look after you." "Thank you girls, you're the best pals I have ever had in my whole life, God bless you both."

Maria closed her eyes. Sarah put her head down to Maria's chest and listened for her Breathing, she raises her head and looks at Claire. "She's gone." Claire asks, what do you mean she's gone?" "Maria has passed away."

Claire gave out a massive scream. "Oh no, not Maria, she's my best friend." Sarah took hold of her, "we did all that we could, I think her poor old heart just gave out at the end.

Would you like some time on your own with her. I'll go and find Doctor Peter, the priest and bring them back to you."

"Yes please, I would like a little time on my own with her and I know she would of loved to be blessed by the priest."

Linda left the room and walked slowly around the hospital to find Peter and the priest. She wanted Claire to spend some time with her friend alone so she could grieve quietly. She knew that like all other typhoid victims, Maria's body would have to-be burnt immediately.

It was a very sad day for Sarah and Claire, Maria would be sadly missedas she had a fantastic personality and would soon cheer you up any time you were feeling a little down.

Later that evening, whilst all the children were in bed and all fast asleep, Peter and Sarah were sitting in front of the fire snuggled up to each other. Sarah asked him, "can I ask you something?" "He replies of course you can, what's up." "Well Peter if you get a chance could you ask Governor Foster about Claire Marchant. She works very hard working with the typhoid victims. May be she could work for us looking after the children with me. We have taken a few more children in, and I know she is a person we can trust. I know she is a prisoner but maybe the Governor might just show a little bit of clemency for her as she has been working with the typhoid patients."

He looks at Sarah and gives one of his cheeky smiles, then told her , "I'll see what he says and don't forget Sarah we have that meeting with the council in a few days."

CHAPTER FIFTEEN

THE MEETING WITH THE COUNCIL

Peter and Sarah are sitting outside the Sydney council committee meeting room. The door to the committee room opens , a doorman acknowledges them and asks would you like to come into the meeting, "please take a seat at the rear of the room". the doorman tells them, which they did.

They looked around the meeting room which was full of large paintings of gentry from the past and a very large painting of the king of England. The room was full of men all dressed in their smart suits with smart white shirts and a very smart committee tie to match.

Among the committee members where Governor's Foster and Spikesley who were both sitting on the top table of five including the vicar and one other man. The rest of the committee members sat around tables facing the top table .

Governor Foster looks down on his agenda and then reads from it, "right, gentlemen next on the agenda is to discuss arranging some funds to help in the finance of Doctor Peter KINGSWOOD who has very kindly set up his home to look after orphaned children, mainly caused by the outbreak of Typhoid Fever. He has been financing this out of his own savings, but he has told me his money will run out soon. So he is looking for some help from us."

A committee member stands and speaks, "I would like to thank the Doctor for his help in this matter but I do not think in my opinion that we would be able to help in anyway shape or form . We have a lot more urgent things at the moment, to spend our money on."

Another member stands up and speaks, "I would also like to thank the Doctor for his kindness to these children, but I must agree with the man speaking before me, we can't just start giving out money here and there."

Sarah stands up and addresses the meeting, "please sirs may I be permitted to speak on behalf of the children."

A committee member ask Sarah, "Who might you be madam." "Sir, I am a nurse at the hospital and the doctor and I will be married one day. Between us we run our home for the poor unfortunate orphaned children. We are looking after around 17 children at the moment and this number will grow. that's what happens when their parents passed away and they have no relatives and nowhere to go. All of these poor children have been totally traumatised by the loss of their parents due to the typhoid fever outbreak. If you could see the fear in these little children's eyes you would be saddened for their loss. You say you have more urgent things to spend your money on . But please tell me sirs, what could be more pressing than these unfortunate children who have no one? Please tell me sir, who is going to feed them ? who is going to tuck them into bed at night? and who is going to put a bandage on their knee if they fall over and cut themselves? Maybe we can bring two or three children around to your houses to live with you and you can bring them up ? .

Remember sirs, these children are the future of this country that you call Australia. So tell me sir's, can you really put a price on that?"

The room goes silent. The committee all stand up and give Sarah a hearty cheer. Governor Peter Foster gets to his feet then speaks. "Please raise your hand and vote for funds to go to the home for orphaned children. I am going to tell you that I am going to vote YES for the fund to go to the home." The Governor looks over at Sarah, smiles then gives her a little wink of his eye.

Every committee member puts up their hand to vote yes . Governor Foster calls out, "ok that's been passed , we can sort out the money side later."

Doctor Peter stands , "sirs, we would both like to thank you all for your vote , we can now get on with the job in hand"

Sarah and Peter walk out of the meeting room feeling very happy that they can continue with their work with the children. As they walked to back to the hospital Peter said to Sarah, "look over there Sarah, there's a lovely little baker's that has just opened, shall we go in and check it out." "All yes please Peter, I am felling a little hungry," She tells him. As they walk though the front door, "there is a fantastic smell of fresh bread baking." They looked at one another and smiled. The man who was the baker looked over the counter at them and said, "yes how may I help you today."   Peter looked into the glass counter where the baker had just put some hot fresh meat and potato pies .

He asked Sarah , "well look at those lovely fresh pie's, would you like one of those," she replies, "yes please, they look delicious." He turned to the baker, "right young man, we would like two of your meat and potato pies please and may we have a pot of tea for two."

The man nods his head and thanks him, "please take a seat and I will bring your food and tea out for you." Peter thanked the man then they sat down.

Peter held Sarah's hand and looked into her eyes, " Your amazing, that speech you gave to the committee was just fantastic, did you rehearse that." She looked at him and smiled, " no it just came from my heart, I wasn't telling any lies, we are not trying to get a financial gain from them, you know these children are genuinely in need of our help."

"Yes I know, there was something else you said in your speech that made me feel very happy. "She frowned at him, not knowing what he was referring to. So she decided to ask him just what he meant by what made him happy? " When you mentioned that one day we would be married." Sarah looked a little shocked, "Oh am so sorry Peter, thinking back on that I should not have said it, I hope I didn't embarrass you, that was so wrong of me, please forgive me."

Peter as usual just laughed, then put out his hand and touched her face with affection.

"Well the reason it made me happy was I would love to marry you Sarah, I have been trying to buck up the courage to ask you for some time now. So what do you think?"

Sarah jumped from her seat and screamed out loud Peter, "YES, YES, YES, of course I'll marry you. He rose to his feet and they embraced. The Baker called out from behind his counter, "Congratulations to you both." Another couple that were sitting near by also waved at them, "yes, Congratulations from us also."

They thanked everyone in the bakery shop for their kind words, finished their pies, drank their tea and left the bakery.

Sarah asked Peter, "can I tell anyone about our engagement." Again he smiled at her, "yes of course you can darling."

.
They walked back to the hospital to check that all was well. He walked off to do his rounds and she walked into the mens ward where nurse Linda was working.

Once nurse Linda saw her she came over and asked how did you get on at the committee meeting," Oh Linda, that worked out just fine, in the end, they have decided to help us financially so we can keep the place going, we are just delighted, l couldn't bear to give up all those beautiful children, they have all just settled in so very well.

I also have some fantastic news to tell you" Linda looked at Sarah perplexed .

"More good news, well please tell me," "My Peter has asked me to marry him." Shegrabbed hold of Sarah and gave her the biggest hug one could ever give. " Oh that's fantastic news,I am so pleased for you both . They then hugged again.

Sarah told her, "I think I'll go and find my other friend Claire Marchant and tell her the good news."

She walked over to Claire in the typhoid tent. As soon as she went in the tent she could see Claire working away with the patient. She called over to her. "Hi Claire when you are free can I have a word please." She looked over and waved, "ok, I'll only be a minute." She called back to her, "I'll see you out side." Once again Claire waves at her.

A few minutes passes by and Claire walks out of the tent to find Sarah standing by the door.

Sarah asks, "How are you." "Not bad, it's been a bit hard the last few weeks since we lost Maria but working here keeps me busy and makes the day go fast. But as there are fewer numbers of people coming into the ward with the typhoid I'll probably have to go back to the prison."

"Well keep this to yourself, I have asked my Peter to have a word with the Governor and see if we can get you out of the prison and help us back at our home that we have created looking after the orphan children."

"My God Sarah, that would be great if you could do that for me. I can't see the Governor standing for it though." Sarah tells her, "well we can only ask. And by the way I have some good news to report to you"

"What's that , I could do with some good news for a change ." "Peter has ask me to marry him." "Jesus Christ, that's brilliant."

They chat for ages, talking about everything and nothing including how she got on with the Sydney council and how they had agreed to fund the orphaned children that she and Peter where bringing up.

Claire asked," do you ever think about England at all." Sarah replies. "Only sometimes,but mainly I think about my my dear mother most day's and twice a day if something happens that reminds me of her, like if it starts raining heavy here and someone starts to moan because I know my dear mum always moaned about the rain." They both started laughing.

Claire says, "right I had better get back to work before I am missed and told off." Sarah agrees, "yes and I'd better get back to work too."

Later that evening after all the children had gone to bed and George and Boo had gone up for the night, Sarah asks to Peter. "There is something that I would like to ask you." Fire away." "Is there a way through any of your contacts in London that I could try to find out how my mother is and tell her that I am ok. I can't stop thinking about her. If you think about it Peter the poor love has had to put up with so much in her life. First my father died and she had to bring us up on her own, the worry about Robert and I then the fact that poor Robert was hung and then me shipped off to the other side of the world as a prisoner probably never to be seen again."

"Yes I agree she must feel devastated to have her whole family ripped apart from her. Ok what I'll do is write too my brother in London and ask him if he can try to find her, when I go to the office tomorrow."" I'll sit down and write a letter with all the facts then take It up to the docks, find the next ship that's going back to England and hopefully we can start the process of finding her. As you know England is a long way and could take months but at least we have made a start."

Sarah puts her arms around him, "I think I am the luckiest women alive to have met someone so kind as you."

As promised the very next day he sat down and composed a letter to his brother. Dear Charles, I hope this letter finds you and the family well, all seems to be ok in Sydney but we have had to deal with an outbreak of typhoid fever. Luckily the Governor here in Sydney took my advice and addressed the situation straight away.

They have completely re channeled all the water systems so there is no chance of cross contamination. Plus he has brought out a new law that all water has to be boiled before drinking.

I now think we have broken the back of the typhoid but we did unfortunately lose quite a few people along the way. Some of them passed away were couple's leaving their children as orphans. Myself and a lovely lady that I met on the way over set up an orphanage as there is no such thing in Australia.

Her name is Sarah and we are engaged to be married. I was wondering Charles, if you could help us out by trying to find Sarah's mother to see if she's ok, arrange for her to travel over to Australia and live with us as she is getting on in her years. I know it would make Sarah so very happy.

I would cover any expenses that you may incur along the way. Her name is Florence Wright. Her last known address was 26, Liverpool road, Islington, Highbury, London.

If you find her please explain that Sarah is fine and settled in Australia and she is to be married me.

Please tell her that we would like her to come to Australia and to live with us. If she says yes to coming to Australia please write back to me straight way so I can make my arrangements as I want to keep it as a surprise for Sarah.

Just let me know what ship you can get her on and the date it will arrive in Australia so I can be there to meet her.

But Charles if you can't find her or she doesn't want to come to Australia, ask her to write a letter about her life and post it to me.

Thank you very much dear brother, I think of you and your lovely family most days.

Kind regards your brother Peter. He seals the letter ready to be sent by ship to England.

Whilst Peter was sitting in his office thinking, there was a knock at the door. He calls out, "it's open, in walked Governors Foster and Spikesley. Peter tells them to take a seat, "may I ask what do I have the pleasure of your visit, Kind sir's."

They say, "as you know we finished all the building works regarding the flowing of fresh water into town and the new trenches to take the sanitation out of town, what we would like to ask you have the cases of typhoid started to slow down, or is it still as bad."

Peter tells them with a smile on his face , "well yes gentlemen it slowed down last week and this week I have not had one case reported to me. So once again I say to you both, "congratulations on your hard work ".

By making it a law that all water has to be boiled it has helped considerably."

Governor Spikesley ask the doctor, "how long do you need the prisoner's that I sent over to help out in the hospital."

"I would think no more than a more month, in fact half can go back in two weeks time."Governor Spikesley nods his head to the doctor, "ok, that's fine as long as I know."

Peter looks at Governor Spikesley and asks him, " sir one of your prisoners,a women called Claire Marchant, is very good with children, so I was wondering if she could come under License and work with us, at what now has become Sydney's first children'sOrphanage."

She would still be a prisoner by law , but she could serve her sentence at the orphanage instead of the prison and would be totally under our control. If she breaks the law in anyway she would have to go back to the prison."

Governor Spikesley replied, "I don't think I would have a problem with that, I will arrange the paperwork for you to sign, if you come over to the prison in a few day's time it will be ready."

"Ok :thank you, is there anything else I can help you with." "No." They replied.

Shook hands and left. Peter walked down to the docks and found a ship going to England that day. He asks one of the crew to direct him to the captain.

He explains to the captain that he is the doctor of the hospital in Sydney and would he post this very important letter when the ship gets back to England.

The captain agrees and will first thing. Peter thanks him.

When he got home that evening all the children were bathed and ready for bed. He tells Sarah, "I am going to help you put the children to bed." "Thank you that will be lovely." Sarah tells him.

Sarah calls out to all the children, "Right every one listen up, Doctor Peter is going to help me take you up to bed so no mucking about,." All the children call out hooray and wereexcited and jumping up and down at the prospect of Peter taking them up to bed.

Slowly they all walked up the stairs one by one, all heading off to their bedrooms, roughly four children to a room. Once all the children where in bed Sarah and Peter went into every room, gave every child a little kiss on the side of their face and tucked all there sheets in so they could snuggle down for a good nights sleep.

Once all the children were settled down, Peter and Sarah came down stairs and settled down on the couch in front of the fire, Peter opened a nice bottle of red wine that he had bought earlier that day, now they could now relax together in front of the fire.

Peter say, "well darling, I must tell you I have had a very fruitful day. She looks at himand asks, "what's happened." "He then tells her, "well my darling both the Governor's came to see me at the hospital this morning. Governor Foster asked me about the typhoid fever out break and do I think that it's started to slow down, i told him yes most definitely and by making it law that everyone must boil their water, it has helped tremendously. He told me all the new trenches had been dugout, fresh water run into town and the new sewage runs away and out into the sea.If the case's start dropping drastically then he will start taking some of the prisoner's that has been helping out at the hospital back to the prison."

Sarah looked at Peter with an anguish look because she was thinking about Claire Marchant who she would of liked to come and work at the orphanage.

Sarah interrupted the conversation and asked Peter with a stern look on her face. "Did you get chance to mention my request about Claire Marchant." " Yes I did." " Well what did they say." "Governor Spikesley said." But then Peter hesitated so he could tease Sarah a little and delay his answer. "Oh come on Peter please don't tease me" He just laughed then told Sarah with a big grin on his face, "yes I did ask Governor Spikesley and he told me that he would release her on licence to serve her sentences with us at the orphanage looking after the children."

Sarah jumped up and down with excitement. "That's fantastic news, you're such a tease."

They just sat back in their chairs sipping their wine and chatting to each other. "And most importantly Sarah I wrote a nice letter to my brother back in England asking him to go to the address you gave me in Highbury, London, to find what he could regarding your dear mother. He knows my address here to write back to me as soon as he knows anything. I actually took the letter myself down to the docks and gave it to the captain of a ship that was leaving for England that day I asked him to post it when they arrive back in England."Peter, you will never know just how grateful I am."

CHAPTER SIXTEEN

THE LETTER THAT WAS SENT TO ENGLAND

Back in London Peter's brother and his family are sitting around the dinning table eating their evening meal and chatting, when his wife tells Charles. "Oh, sorry I should of told you earlier, "a letter came for you today, I've put it on the on your desk, shall I go and get it for you." "Yes please Mary,"off she goes, brings the letter to him. He opens the envelope and carefully and reads the letter.

"My God it's from my dear brother Peter in Australia." "Is every thing ok, Charles"

"Yes, yes, he is fine, In fact his got engaged, it appears he met a nurse, her name is Sarah and he would like me to go up to Highbury to see if I could try and find her mother and possibly make some arrangements for the woman to go to Australia to live with them."

Mary replies, " Very interesting." Charles say's, "yes, that's what I thought. He must love the woman and I am very happy for him. Let me see, it's Thursday today, I'll go to Highbury on Saturday and see what I can find out. May be you would like to come with me."

"Yes, ok that might be a good idea because a woman will open up to another woman."

On Saturday, bright and early Charles and Mary are up and ready to go. Their home is in Holborn, which as the crow flies, is only a few miles from Highbury. They walk a few hundred yards from their house when a horse driven cab comes along. Charles raises his arm to make the cab driver aware that they require his services.

The cab stops and Charles helps his wife into the carriage and gets in calling out to the cabby, "please take us to 26, Liverpool Road, Highbury, Islington." The driver touches his hat to acknowledge that he has heard the address and off they go, straight towards Angel Islington then turning left at upper street into Liverpool road. The cab driver slowed down so he could see the numbers of the houses. Then drove along Liverpool road for around five minutes and there it was, number twenty six, the cab driver pulled up right out side. Charles got out first and helped Mary out. He paid the cab driver his fare and the cab drove off.

Charles and Mary stood outside the house for a few moments, it was a four story house that Had been converted into small flats . They both walked up the path to the front door.

It hadn't been painted for years. They could see the front step had been painted in red and was spotlessly clean. There was a big black iron door knocker which Charles banged on. No one came so Charles knocked again, this time a little harder. A window on the upper floor opened and a woman popped her head out.

She called down to them, "yes what do you want." Charles called back to her, "do you have a Mrs Florence Wright living here". "Yes we do, she lives down stairs, I'll go down and see If she is in co's she doesn't always open the door these days." "OK, that's fine, thank you."

About five minutes passed by before the door opened. This time a different woman opens the door" "Yes, I am Flory Wright what do you want. I ain't got any money if that's what your after."

Charles tells her, "it's about Sarah, that I believe is your daughter." "Did you say Sarah my daughter. Please come in . Let's go into my flat where it's private and we can talk. Please sit down." Mrs Wright looks directly at Charles with a stern face, then asks, "what's happened to my Sarah" is she ok."

Charles replies with a gently tone to his voice as he does not want her to feel intimidated .

He starts by telling her that he has received a letter from his brother who is a Doctor in the hospital in Sydney ,Australia. He then goes on to say, "Firstly your daughter Sarah is fine and is doing well."

Mrs Wright fell from her chair onto the floor, then screams out loudly, "Thank God for that I pray for her every day. She is such a wonderful child, kind thoughtful, and loving and how she got sent to Australia as a prisoner for such a petty thing is unbelievable." Mary got up from her seat and walked over to her and helped her off the floor , so she could sit back down again on her wooden chair.

Charles tell's Mrs Wright. "To be honest, we are both here because my brother Peter wrote to me asking to try and find you, firstly tell you that Sarah is safe and well and theyare engaged to be married. They have opened an orphanage for young children and would like you to go over to Australia, live with them and help in the orphanage if you wanted too."

Mrs Wright again scream's out but this time with laughter. "What me go to Australia I can't even afford to get on a bus to the shops let alone Australian in fact I had never heard of Australia until my Sarah got transported off there."

"Peter my brother will pay for your trip to Australia. I can tell you that they are really keen for you to go." "Well it all sounds very nice Flory tells them but I wouldn't even know how to book such a trip. To be honest Mr Charles I ain't ever been out of this Islington . I went up the West End a few years ago but that's about all."

"Look, if you're prepared to go I'll arrange everything, a carriage will pick you up from your home and take you to the ship direct, once you have boarded the ship you will be shown to your own cabin. Then when you get to Australia you will be met at the docks, probably by Peter. So you haven't got to worry about anything " "Are you sure this isn't a joke or your kidding me on."Flory asks.

"No Mrs Wright this isn't a joke, I am very serious about what I am telling you."

"My brother and I are very close I would do anything to help him as he would for me and that's the only reason my wife and I are here today."

"Well Mr Charles, I also would do anything for my Sarah, and the chance of putting my arms around her and holding her tight once again would be fantastic. I thank you both for coming to see me and letting me know that Sarah is alright. That means everything to me. Please Mr Charles I don't want to take liberties but I haven't got any clothes to wear. For such a trip. Times have been very hard for me and most of my clothes are old and faded."

Charles laughed gently, "Mrs Wright, please don't worry about a thing. I will come over and see you next Saturday midday and we can discuss the trip again." I will start making some inquiries re the trip.

That week just flew past for Charles as he was trying to arrange the trip for Mrs Wright. He found a ship that was travelling to Australia in two weeks time, the next one after that was in six weeks. He told the travel company that he would let them know which ship she would go on after he had discussed the situation with Mrs Wright.

Like Charles promised, he went to Mrs Wright's flat in Highbury the following Saturday. He knocked at the door but this time Mrs Wright opened the door straight away. "Hello Mr Charles, please come in." They both walked into the flat and sat down.

Charles Starts to tell Mrs Wright, "there's a ship going to Sydney in two weeks time, what do you think." "Yes please Mr Charles that sounds good to me." She replies. " I know I mentioned it last week to you and your dear wife, but I haven't got any clothing to wear, I mean I don't want anything posh or expensive but the clothing I do have is old and shabby. It's all clean and washed but I only have a couple of cleaning jobs which don't pay a lot of money."

"Ok, don't worry, I'll bring Mary with me next Saturday and she will take you shopping to buy some new clothing for the journey, how's that."

"Oh my God it is true then I am going to Australia." Charles looks at her and smiles, "yes Mrs Wright, you are going to Australia and you will soon be back with your Sarah." Mrs Wright could not contain herself as she ran the length of the front room and put her arms around Mr Charles body then hug him so tight , and couldn't stop thanking him.

Mr Charles could see the funny side of it and laughed out loud himself.

"Let's confirm your arrangements. The ship will be leaving in just under two week from today. Next Saturday I will bring you all your travel details plus your tickets. Mary my wife will take you to get some nice new clothing for the trip, how's that." "That great Mr Charles, I still have to pinch myself every day to prove that it's not a dream."

"So all we want you to do is relax, figure out what personal effects that you want to take with you, Mary and I will help you get packed. We will also be here to see you off on the day you leave. That way we know all's well."

"O thank you Mr Charles, you are so kind, if your brother is like you my Sarah will be a very lucky girl." Charles smiled at her then told her, "believe me my brother is a very nice man."

The next Saturday soon came round when Charles and Mary were at the door of Mrs Wright's in Liverpool road. All three of them sat in the front room, Charles opened a large envelope containing all of Mrs Wright's Travel documents. "These are your boarding passes for the ship, here is your passport document, and this is your cabin number. While you're on board ship there is breakfast , lunch, and dinner. These will be served in the dinning room each day. There's nice big decks for you to walk and exercise on, a few shops, and a doctor in the sick bay should you need it."

"I have posted a letter to my brother giving him your travel detail's so he can be at the harbour to meet you on your arrival."

"My God Mr Charles, it seems so exciting, I was very nervous at the prospects of it all but now I am so looking forward to the journey and meeting my Sarah again."

Mary then told her, "OK, shall we go down to the West End and buy you a couple of trunks and some nice clothing for day and evening wear." Flory smiled, then burst into tears .

"I am so sorry. No one has ever shown me so much kindness before, After my husband died all those year's ago I had to spend every penny I earned on trying to bring up the children.There was never anything left for me, even when the children were gone, I just didn't have the strength or the courage to pick myself up again."

Mary replied, "well all of that is about to change now. Once you get to Australia you'll be back with your daughter and you can start a fresh new life."

"Thank you so much Mary for those kind words." "That's OK, let's get a cab, drop Charles off and go to the West End and do some shopping."

It only took a few minutes to stop a cab in Liverpool road as it was always very busy, once the women had dropped Charles at his home they told the cabby, "please take us to Oxford street." They had a wonderful time looking in all the different shops at the vast collection of clothing , with Mary picking out the garments that she thought was right for Mrs Wright to wear on her voyage. They looked at all the piles of clothing they had bought from underwear to gowns, from slippers to high heels , everything was now in place. They needed not two trunks but five for the amount they had brought.

A man from from the last shop they went into walked outside the the store and stopped two cabs. One for the ladies and one for the luggage and clothing. Mary then suggested they should make a new plan, "Let's take all these goods back to my house and you can stay with us for the last week and we can have a lot of fun with you dressing up in your new clothing.

We can go to your flat and pick up any other bits that you want to take. Then next Saturday you can leave for the docks from our house, what do you think."

She replies, " I must say that seems a fabulous idea, but I don't want to put you out in any way ,you have both been so kind to me and I am so grateful, you will never know."

Mary gently laugh's then tells her."Don't be silly, we both think that you are a lovely woman and although we do not know all the sad details about your family we can tell that your heart is in the right place , so you come home with us so we can make sure you're on the right track to go off to Australia for your new life."

The last week before Mrs Wright leaves for Australia just flew by. She had picked up a few personal possessions from her flat in Liverpool Road, like photos of her family and odd bits of cheap jewellery that had sentimental value.

Early Saturday morning everything was ready. The trunks were packed Mrs Wright was dressed in her new clothing ready for her journey. "Please let me thank you both from the bottom of my heart , I can honestly say that I will never forget you both for your kindness and help."

Her carriage turned up dead on time. All of her possessions were loaded on board then they all walked out ready for her to leave. She asked them both, "please may I give you both a big hug and kiss for all that you have done for me, I will tell your brother Peter and my Sarah just how kind you have been to me."

She hugged and kisses them both, as she got into the carriage that would take her to the docks and off to Australia as the carriage pulled away Flory waved from the carriage window with tear of joy in her eyes.

CHAPTER SEVENTEEN

SARAH BOO AND CLAIRE TAKE THE CHILDREN TO THE PARK

All the children are on a break from their schools Sarah decided to take them to Waverley park in Sydney that was around a ten minute walk away from their house. Sarah, Claire and Boo made up some sandwiches and drinks for the children. Off they all marched down the road. Sarah went first then some children then Boo in the middle, followed by more children and Claire at the end. That way they couldn't lose any of the children on the way.

Once at the park Sarah set out some big rugs so they could all sit together and eat a bit later after the children had a nice time playing all together.

All the children were running around laughing and having a wonderful time. Sarah and Claire where talking together when they saw a horse and carriage driving near to them.

As the carriage got nearer it started to slow down and stop. The windows of the carriage where darkened so that no one could see who was sitting in side.but the person sitting inside could see out.

After around ten minutes or so a man got out of the carriage and started to walk towards them. By now all the children were sitting on the large rug that they had taken to the park. Sarah, Boo and Claire where busy sorting out the food for the children to eat.

Sarah looked up as the man got closer and could see he was wearing a very smart uniform.

But she did not want to be rude and just star at the man so she just looked at the children and out of the corner of her eye she could see if the man was actually walking towards her and the children. Suddenly the man stopped right in front of Sarah,

Sarah looked up and smiled at the man, she now recognised who it was, it was in fact Peter Foster the Governor of Sydney and New South Wales.

Sarah stood up immediately, then greeted him with a hand shake. "Well good morning Governor, how nice to see you, especially on such a lovely warm day."

"Thank you Miss Wright and yes it is a lovely day. I was just driving through the park when I noticed you your helper's and the children, I must say just how happy you all look especially the children. I was only the other day, telling my wife what a marvellous job you were doing. Now looking back at the situation with the children, God knows what would of happened to them if you and the doctor had not come to the forefront and taken them on, putting them all into your home to look after.

Sarah being Sarah just looked at the Governor then smiled at him. "By the way Miss Wright,is there anything that the council can help you with." Sarah just nodded her head, "no I think we are just fine but thank you so much for your kindness."

"No Miss Wright, It's you and the doctor who we should thank for your kindness." The Governor replies

She looks at the children then asks them to all stand up, even the little ones. All the children do as Sarah asked, "Right children, this gentlemen is the Governor of Sydney and has been very kind to us all by supporting our home where we all live so please would you all step over to him and shake him by the hand and tell him, Thank you sir." They did this one by one. She could tell by the Governors face just how touched he was by this deed.

He tells Sarah, "well I suppose I must get back to work even though it has been just so nice talking to you, watching the children play and look so happy especially after what trauma they have been though."

She asks the Governor, "sir please may I walk with you to your carriage. "Off course you can, it will be an absolute pleasure." As they both walked back to the carriage they both made small talk to one another.

The Governor asks her, "don't forget if there is anything I can ever do for you, even on a personal note, just let me know."

She looked into the air, then asked the Governor. "Please Governor, there is just one thing I would like to ask you." "Fire away" he replies, "well Governor as you know the doctor and myself hope to get married in the near future, so would it be cheeky of me to ask you,would you consider giving me away on our big day. My poor dad passed away when I was very young and your such a kind man and now a good friend of the family that it would be such an honour for you to give me way

The Governor looked totally elated. His reply was "of course I will . It will be a pleasure and honour." She thanked the Governor as he climbed into his carriage, he then called out to his driver, "Government house please driver."Off the carriage went out of the park.

Sarah, Boo, Claire and the children had a wonderful day at the park and couldn't wait to tell Peter as he walked into the house.

Later that evening Sarah and Peter sat relaxing in the parlour like they did most evenings. sipping a small glass of red wine and talking about their day.

She told him, "well guess who I had a nice conversation with today." He looked mystified as to who it could have been putting a frown upon his face.

Sarah carried on, "well it was the Governor, Peter Foster. He was driving through Waverley park today and saw myself with Claire, Boo and the children. He told me just how pleased he was at the way we were looking after the children, He also told me if there was anything he could do for us either financially or personally to let him know."

He asked her, "what was your reply." " I asked him one thing he might consider as a private matter." "what was that" he asked, "I asked the Governor to give me away on our wedding day."

Peter roared with laughter. "So tell me what did he say." She smiled at him, "well he said it will be a pleasure to do such a thing and an honour."

Peter told her, "darling you're just amazing, specially all the hard work that you have put in, to firstly the hospital, then the children, is fantastic. I have never meet such a dedicated person in all my life."

She asked Peter, " I know it was quite some time since you had written to your brother about trying to trace my mother. But did you ever get any news back from England "regarding my mother." "Not yet" he told her, it's still early days so much time has passed us by, she must of moved and my brother may have trouble trying to find her."

"Yes that's true." She replies, "I do hope he can find her even if it is only to tell her I am ok". "Yes, I know what you mean. It must be horrible for your mother not knowing what became of you."

But what Sarah didn't know was that Peter had indeed heard from his brother by a letter that was delivered to the hospital a few days ago. The letter read "Hello Peter, I have found your Sarah's mother. She still lives in her little flat in Liverpool road, In Islington. My wife and I had a good talk to her, we told her that Sarah is well and doing ok. And I must say she was generally over whelmed and glad of the news about her daughter I have told her about the fact that you and Sarah are going to marry at some point, and that you would like her to be at the wedding, to stay and live with you both in Australia, Peter she was very nervous to start with but I think her confidence has come back to her slightly. She has told me that she would like to take up your kind offer, and come to Australia and live with you both.

We have booked her onto a passenger ship bound for Australia. All the dates are listed here in this letter. The name of the ship date it leaves England and the date the ship arrives in Sydney. Please make sure you are at the dock to meet her as I have saidshe is not a confident woman. In our opinion she is a very nice and honest lady who's poor heart has been destroyed by the events that have gone on.

We are keeping well, the new job that I took in the city is working out very well, I enjoy the job immensely. The people that I work with are all very nice which as you know helps.

Please keep me in informed how things work out with Mrs Wright and how your wedding goes.

P.s stay safe and look forward to reading your next letter to us.

Regards, Charles.and Mary.

Peter was very excited by his brother's letter about Sarah's Mum travelling to Australia. Hethought this will be the best wedding gift anyone could ever give to someone, especially to the love of his life Sarah. Even though Peter was a little worried about Sarah's reaction and hoped that it would not come as a shock that could back fire on him.

A few weeks soon past by when Governor Foster came to visit Doctor Peter at the hospital, Peter asks him, "would you like to come into our canteen to eat and talk at the same time. "

Yes that's a good idea, let's go."Once in the canteen they sat down at a table and started to talk. He asked Peter,"have you and Sarah set a date for your wedding yet." "Yes I went down to the church the other day and discuss the matter with the vicar and we have sorted out a date it's going to be on Saturday the fifteenth of June. I believe you have kindly agreed to give Sarah away.""Yes

I have." He said, "and Peter I am really looking forward to it."

Peter then told the Governor about Sarah's mother and how his brother Charles had contacted her by driving up to the last known address in Islington London. luckily enough she was still living at the same address. Sarah's mother was so pleased that Sarah was alive and well.

"So my brother has arranged a ship for her to come over to Australia and be at the wedding. I haven't told Sarah, I am keeping it as a surprise for her on our wedding day give me your thoughts on that if you don't mind?"

He told him, "to be truthful Peter what I would do is get her mother over in Australia, then arrange a meeting between them in a hotel a few days before the wedding so on the wedding day it doesn't come as a total shock to her as she could be overcome and spoil the day." Peter thought long and hard for a moment then he replies, "Governor, you know that good sound advice and that's exactly what I shall do."

The Governor told Peter, "what about if I walk into the room with Sarah's mother by my side and I am there with you for the big surprise." "What a fantastic idea Governor, at least my good intentions can't back fire on me. " He smiled at Peter and replies, "exactly." Peter tells the Governor "I'll get it all organised and let you know the time and the place. " He replies. "That sounds good to me." They shake hands and part company.

A week before Mrs Wright arrives , Peter goes to the Grand Hotel In Sydney that is near to The harbour so when Sarah's mother arrives she will have some where to stay that is very nice and comfortable for her. Even though it will only be for about five days, that way she can rest after her long journey and settle in then Peter can arrange the surprise for Sarah.

CHAPTER EIGHTEEN

MRS WRIGHT ARRIVES IN AUSTRALIA

Peter is up bright and early on the morning that Mrs Wright's ship is due to arrive in the harbour. Sarah, Claire and Boo all come down stairs with the children. Sarah tells Peter, "I didn't hear you get up this morning." He smiles and tells her, "I have a lot to do today." "OK, anything special." "Not really but I want to go into the hospital nice and early so I can check my paperwork then do my rounds. I need to go off to Sydney to the Harbour to pick up some new equipment for the hospital that I ordered to come by ship from England. I don't want it to go missing for weeks on end so it is important that I personally collect it.

"Peter, why don't you just send George to collect the equipment by doing that you will save Yourself the worry of travelling in to Sydney."

"No, I want to check the equipment myself as its very special and I don't want anything to go wrong."

"OK, you know what you are doing this equipment must be very special.""Trust me Sarah it is."

Peter makes his way down to the harbour in Sydney. Mrs Wright ship was now in the harbour but no one had disembarked yet. He stood there watching the ship with baited breath. He can hear sailor's shouting from the ship then all of a sudden a gang plank started to come off the ship. Two sailors on the ground took a hold of it and secured it fast to an anchor point on the ground. The sailors secured the hand rails each side of the gang plank so it was safe for people to disembark. Crowds of passengers were ready to get off the ship. Slowly, they started to walk down the gangway of the ship and onto the harbour dock. There was lots of people standing and watching the crowds of people walking down onto the dock then running up to them and hugging them.

After around ten minutes or so Peter could see a middle aged women walking down the gangway on her own. When she was off the gang way and standing alone in the harbour, he decided to approach her.

"Excuse me madam, are you Mrs Wright by any chance." "Yes I am, may I ask you who you are." Peter replies by telling her. "I am Doctor Peter KINGSWOOD, your Sarah's Fiancée." " Oh it's so nice to meet you after all this time" Florence tell him, you are a very handsome man indeed." She told him in her cockney accent? .Peter laughed. "You're just as your Sarah described you."

He called the porter over and asked him to load Mrs Wright's luggage onto his horse and carriage that he had waiting. He called up to the carriage driver. "Please take us to the grand hotel." the driver nodded his head and off they trotted at a steady pace.

Mrs Wright just couldn't help herself but look out off the window as everything looked so much different than

England. All the buildings had corrugated tin roofs some buildings were made with dark red bricks others were made of timber and most of them had metal balustrades and, verandas wrapped around the buildings . People seemed to be dressed in a total different way to what they were in England.

The carriage soon stopped outside The Grand Hotel in Sydney. A man from the hotel came running out with a wooden set of steps which he put by the door of the carriage to make it easier for the passengers to get out from the carriage. Peter got out first then raised his hand to help Mrs Wright out of the carriage so she did not have a accident. The porter from the hotel then took in the luggage into the foyer of the hotel .

Peter went to the reception desk where a smart man stood ready to book Mrs Wright in.

Peter explains to the man, "sir I have made a reservation for this lady to stay here at your hotel." The receptionist says, "that fine sir, please may I ask the ladies name , Peter replies it's Mrs F Wright. Her ship has just docked at the harbour, I made a reservation for her to stay here for five days." And Peter tells the receptionist "I want this lady well looked after, anything she wants if it's in your power you must get it for her, do you understand me."

"Yes of course sir, I understand." And Peter tells the receptionist. "I will be settling her bill at the end of her stay."

The receptionist writes down her details then asks Mrs Wright to sign the register, which she does, A porter is called and the luggage is taken up to her room which is number Fifteen.

Peter then asks the receptionist, "sir can we have some lunch." "Of course you can sir and madam, I'll take you both into the dining room." They sat down and Peter ask" Florence would you like to look at the menu ", Florence just stared at Peter, "to be honest Peter I have never been in a hotel or a restaurant before in my whole life, so I wouldn't know what I was looking at ?, what did you call it a menu, or something like that.

Peter just smiles at Florence then hold's her hand for a few seconds. "Don't you worry Florence tell me do you like lamb chops, ""once again Florence whispers to Peter " well if you recommend them , I'll eat them cos I never tasted them before" Peter cal's the waiter over. "Sir we would like to order the lamb chops please plus roast potatoes and some vegetables and that's for both off us,". Peter also tells the waiter " please bring us a bottle of your best red wine and two glasses please." The waiter says, " of course sir."

Mrs Wright then asked Peter . "Please before we go any further my first name is Florence, but I like to be called Flory in England everyone who knows me calls me Flory

He tells her, "Flory it is then. "I haven't told your Sarah that you are here in Australia, thought I would keep it for a nice surprise for her. I was going to spring it on her at the church as her wedding gift, but a friend of mine told me that it might come as too much of a shock on the day. So what I thought was we will give you some time for you to settle down, then on Thursday I'll bring Sarah to the hotel for lunch and you can walk in to the lounge with my friend and surprise her.

Flory says, "I hope you don't mind me asking but what shall I call you, would it be Doctor Peter , Peter, or Mr Kingswood, as I have never been in this position before. living in London we just call every one by their first name, unless it's someone posh."

"Flory please just call me Peter , Christ you will be my mother in law soon."They both started laughing so loud that other people eating in the restaurant looked over at them.

After lunch Peter said, "right I'll come up to your room with you and get you all settled in." "Ohthank you Peter that will be nice." When they got to room number fifteen they opened thehotel door and walked in , Flory asked him, "well this cannot be my room." Peter answered, "why yes Flory, it's is your room, why what's wrong with it ."

She just looked around the room with amazement , "I don't mean that I don't like It, I think it's too posh for someone like me. Peter I would like to explain something to you, sadly for no fault of my own I have not particularly had a good life .

My poor beautiful husband died when the children where young , I didn't want to bring any other man into the children's life, it never works out. So the little money I did earn went to feed us all and pay the rent on our little flat in Islington. I brought the children odd bits of clothing. Sarah worked doing odd jobs which brought in some money that helped out. But with reference to myself I only had hand me downs in clothing and shoes because there was nothing left to buy myself anything . The only reason I have these nice cloths now is because your wonderful brother and his wife bought them for me and the trip over.

I lost my husband, then I lost my beautiful young son to the hang man through a wicked judge who could have shown some mercy but chose not to.

The judge then sent my Sarah far across the world away from me. I am an honest women, hard working and kind but who cares no one.

That's why when I am given something like this beautiful room and nice clothes I am waiting for someone to take it away from me . I get frightened."

"Please believe me Flory ," Peter takes her hand and holds it tight. "This is your room, the best in the hotel and it's yours for as long as you stay here. All the nice clothes you now have are yours. No one will ever take them away from you, and Sarah and I want you to live the rest of your life at our home in Australia. You are now a part of the KINGSWOOD family. I promise you here and now you will be loved and be happy with us for the rest of your day's."

Flory just broke down and cried. Peter cradled her in to his chest and waited patiently for her to stop.

Peter told her, "right Flory let's make a plan. Tomorrow I will send a family friend around to meet you. She is a lovely lady that helps out in the hospital, her name is Katie Crowhurst . I will get her to come to the hotel tomorrow, say around ten a.m. She will take you clothes shopping. Let's see if we can get you a lovely dress for our wedding day and a beautiful new hat to match. What do you think." "Bless you Peter for all your kindness and lovely words . To be honest, for the first time in my life I am totally speechless."

Peter gave her a gentle smile and told her, "I can't wait to see Sarah's face when you too meet up again. Right, I had better get back to work at the hospital. If you need anything just let Katie know and she will organise it for you. Don't forget this Saturday it's our wedding day. Katie on the day will collect you and bring you to the church. After the wedding you will be coming back to our house to live with us forever. On Thursday at twelve o'clock my friend Governor Foster will come to your room and walk with you to the restaurant in the hotel where I will be sitting with your Sarah, OK."

"Yes I totally understand, I'll be ready and once again thank you."

As planned Katie Crowhurst called at the hotel for Flory, She took her around all the lovely women's clothing shops in Sydney, where they purchased everything that she could ever need for the wedding and much more.

After their shopping trip Katie asked Flory if she would like to have afternoon tea and some cake. Flory soon agreed, afternoon tea she thought God that's a first. They both walked into a little homemade bakery and sat down , it wasn't long before a large woman asked them, "what would you like madam ". in a English accent Flory eyes open wide, Flory asked the lady, can you repeat that, once again she asked , what would you like madam, tea ?. Flory looked at the women smiled at her and asked, excuse me miss but is that an English accent I can here.

"Yes ". she replies, "well so do I "Fflory told the women Flory carried on I have just come to Australia a few days ago from a place called Islington in London, do you know it. The women then called out to her husband, George, George come here , he walked over with a big frown on his head , what's up?. Well you're not believe this but the lady has just come to Australia from Islington in London. George the baker calls out well we come from Bethnal Green thats about ten minutes from you, well what a small bloody world it's getting.So what brings you to Australia then my girl. Well Flory tells them I am here to go to my Daughters' wedding next Saturday then I am going to live with them in Sydney my daughter is a nurse and my son in law is the Doctor at Sydney hospital.

Well my lovely the tea and some nice freshly baked cake is on us for you and your friend.

Once you have settled down you bring your daughter into our bakery to meet us. It's nice to here a English accent now and again.

Both Katie and Flory enjoy their refreshments and Flory promises to return.

CHAPTER NINETEEN

THE DAY SARAH MEETS HER MOTHER

Thursday seemed to come around in a flash, Flory did not sleep well the night before the reunion as the excitement of being reunited with her daughter after all this time was over whelming.

On Thursday morning Flory hopped out of her bed and pulled back the curtains.

Already she could see it was going to be a nice hot day. As she looked out of the window and could see just how busy the streets were with people going about their business of the day. Flory looked at the big church across the way where she could see the clock on top of the steeple. It was now eight thirty five, her mind went into over drive. Christ, she thought only another three and a half hours and Peter's friend will be knocking on the door, I'd better make a start to get myself ready.

Flory got out all of her nice clothing starting with her panties, stockings, shoes, a beautiful frock, and a nice top to match her frock. She laid them out on her bed, stood back and admired them. She looked hard and thought, you know I think there's something missing. She frowned, as she could not work out what was missing, Then it came to her, YES ,YES , I got it, where's my bonnet that matches my frock and top,

She went to her wardrobe and there it was sitting on the top shelf waiting for her. She got herself bathed and put her hair up in a beautiful bun that was quite fashionable at that time, walked over to her bed and started to dress, nice and slowly, as she didn't want anything to go wrong.

Bit by bit she got dressed each peace matching in every way, looked in the mirror admiring herself as she went. Once finished Flory looked in the mirror again thinking to herself, o my god who's that lady in the mirror looking back at me , it can't be me she looked again into the mirror then pinched herself hard it is me and no this isn't a dream.

Then out of the blue there was a loud knock at the door, she rushed to the window and looked at the church clock it was twelve o'clock exactly. And that was the time that Peter's friend Peter Foster was coming to get her and take her down to the restaurant in the hotel.

She walked across the room and opened the door. There in front of her stood a tall smart man dressed in a nice uniform. He spoke first, "excuse me madam are you Mrs Wright by any chance". "Yes I am, please come in." Flory put out her hand and shook the hand of the Governor.

She said, "it's very nice to meet you sir but may I ask your name." Yes of course, myname is Peter Foster, I am the Governor of New South Wales and a friend of Doctor

Peter KINGSWOOD and Sarah. In fact it will be me that is giving your daughter away on their wedding day."

Flory replies, "thank you for that. Sarah's father died unfortunately many years ago. Please will you take a seat sir while I put my bonnet on, I promise I'll only be a few minutes.

He tells her, "of course, please take your time."

Peter and Sarah had by now arrived at the hotel and were being seated in the restaurant.

Sarah said, "well I must say darling this is a nice surprise, I can't remember the last time we ate out and only two days to our wedding day," "Yes Sarah, I hope you don't mind but I have arranged a little surprise for you."

She looked very perplexed at the thought of a surprise, she was thinking to herself, a ring or maybe a broach. "OK Peter, that's very nice of you, will I get the surprise before or after lunch."

"Hopefully before lunch, in a few more minutes I hope." Then right on cue the door opens and in walked he Governor and Mrs Wright.

Mrs Wright had her bonnet pulled over slightly to one side of her face. They walked up to where Peter and Sarah where sitting .Peter's heart by now was pounding.

Sarah's eyes opened wide as she looked at the pair of them. The Governor spoke first, "Good afternoon Sarah." "Good afternoon Governor, what a nice surprise seeing you here"

"Yes indeed Sarah." Mrs Wright lifted her bonnet rim so it was straight allowing her face to be shown . The Governor spoke out with a grin on his face, "please may I introduce a friend of mine." Sarah smiled at the Governor, "Yes of course you may." Mrs Wright firstly removed her bonnet and looked directly at Sarah. Sarah frowned then slightly nodded her head, "I think I know you but for the moment I don't know who."

Flory Wright gave out the loudest laugh Sarah rolled her eyes. But before could say anything Flory asked. "Don't you recognise me darling, it's your mum all dressed up in me fancy clothing."

Sarah dropped the glass of wine that she was holding, in shock and jumped out off her seat nearly falling over as she did so.

"Mum, mum, is it really you." They grabbed hold of each other hugging and kissing.

The tears just rolling down their faces. Sarah stepped back to take a second look,"Yes it's you my darling, I just can't believe it." They both hugged and screamed out again.

A couple on another table looked over and smiled as they could see just how happy the two of them were.

After around five minutes of laughing and crying at the same time, Sarah turned to Peter and asked him . "Did you organise this." He looked straight into her eyes then told her. "Yes darling I did, I thought it would be a nice surprise for you as your wedding gift."

She put her arms around him and gave him the biggest hug and kiss you could ever imagine ." And as for you Governor, I can't believe you were in on this secret as well." She threw her arms around the Governor as well, then kissed him gently on the side of the face,

He told Sarah, "To be honest I only knew a couple weeks ago, that's when Peter told me. He in fact wanted to save the surprise until the day of the wedding, in the church, but I thought it could back fire on him if the shock was too much on the day. So we discussed it and he agreed it was sensible to have the meeting a few days before, so that's why we are here."

"But tell me Peter how did you organise for my mum to get here." "Well Sarah, it was my brother Charles and his wife that did all of that for me back in England.Firstly they found your mum still living in the same flat in Liverpool road, Islington and organised the ship. Hence she is here for our wedding and to live with us for ever and a day."

"But you never said anything to me about that, I am amazed that you could keep a secret so long," She started to laugh, "your just an amazing person, thank you."

She asks Peter, "can't we take mum home today." "Look, Sarah with the wedding day coming up the day after tomorrow there's still bits and pieces that we need to sort out and I have arranged for Katie Crowhurst to come to the hotel tomorrow, take your mum around Sydney, then on Saturday she will collect her and bring her to the church.

Sarah asks her mother, "darling are you ok with that." She replies, "yes of course I am andwhen am I living with you and Peter we will have all the time in the world to chat and tell me about your amazing adventure."

"Ok darling, if your happy then so am I, let's eat, enjoy the day and our time together." The Governor spoke. "I'll drink to that," Everyone by now was happy and laughing. Flory sat next to her Sara, when they weren't eating they both hugged each other and held hands . They decided not to talk about their events in life as they did not want to get upset. They agreed to leave all off that till sometime after the wedding.

CHAPTER TWENTY

THE WEDDING DAY

There House on that wedding morning was a hive of activity. Children were running around full of excitement. Claire, Boo, and George where chasing after them trying to get them washed, dressed and into their fine clothing for the wedding that day, Peter was upstairs in one bedroom getting ready while Sarah was in the other.

Once they had rounded up the children and got them dressed Claire decided to go upstairs to see if Sarah required any help. "Oh yes please Claire, my hair just seems to be all over the place and I just can't get it to look right.

"Don't worry, have you got any hair pins." Claire asked "Yes I do, over there on that book on the top of the draws." She walks over and picks up pins. "Right sit down on that stool and lets see what we can do." Claire started pulling hair up and pinning it, then pulling it another way and pinning it. After ten minutes Sarah's hair looked brilliant,

She jumped up, looked in the mirror, o Claire that looks just fine I am so happy now."

Sarah walked across the bedroom to the bed where her wedding dress was laying, she picked up the dress and held it up against her body. Claire was watching her every move.

Claire told her "your dress is amazing, I have never seen a wedding dress so lovely. Let's see what it looks like on you." She slid into the dress she, wiggled her body around a bit and the dress just slid into position. Claire walked to the back of Sarah and did up the back fastener's, She told her, "my god, you look like a Queen."

Sarah walked around the room her train just flowed behind her, both women were giggling so loud everyone in the house could hear them.

Peter calls out from the other bedroom, "I say Claire if that's you, please could you come and fix my tie for me."

Ok she shouted out, "I'll be over in one minute." She needed that minute to compose her self. Right Sarah you're ready, I'd better pop next door and sort out Peter's tie." Once that was done Claire ,Boo, and George got ready.

One hour passed when there was a loud knock at the door one of the children ran toopen it. Outside was Governor Joseph Spikesley from the prison.

The Governor walked into the parlour where everyone was waiting except Sarah, who wasupstairs waiting for them all to go to the church with Boo who was her Maid of Honour.

"Good morning everyone." The Governor looked over at Peter . Everyone including the children called back . "Good morning Governor. "

"Ok Peter, are you ready. I have the carriage waiting outside for you to go to the church and two more for the children George and Claire.

Peter calls out , " OK let's go.I'll see you at the church Sarah."

Then turned to Boo and say's, "Please look after my girl and thank you for being our friend . I'll see you all at the church." Governor Peter Foster was outside the church waiting forSarah to arrive.

At the hotel Katie Crowhurst arrived and was in the room with Flory.

Flory had been up a long time, was dressed and ready to go. Katie said, "you look absolutely wonderful Flory, Do you think so." "yes I do." Katie told her.

Flory then says,"you know six months ago before Peter's brother Charles came and found me in my little flat, I had nothing to my name , just some secondhand cloths and some old shoes. I still kept myself lovely and clean but everything was old and washed out."

She jumped to her feet, "BUT TAKE A LOOK AT ME NOW, I feel so happy and I have my beautiful daughter back with me , I thought I had lost her forever."

Katie looked over at her, then holds her hand . "Well I think the only way to look at it is YOUR NEW LIFE STARTS NOW."

"Thank you Katie that makes total sense, you know I never knew such wonderful people existed in this world."

"Ok, let's go and see my beautiful daughter get married." "Yes, I have our carriage waiting right outside the hotel." Down the stairs they walked and into the lobby,

Everyone in the lobby looked at them in their best frocks ready to go to the wedding, Flory smiled to herself as she walked out of the hotel, she felt like the bell of the ball.

Doctor Peter and Governor Joseph Spikesley left for the church in their horse and carriage.

Ten minutes later George and Claire loaded up all the children into two more carriages.

Claire traveled in one and George in the other.

Off they all went off to the church.

Down the stairs walked Sarah with Boo closely behind her holding her train keeping it off the floor. Sarah said, "well it's our time to leave for the the church now." They walked out of the house slowly and into the carriage, Boo keeping a nice tight grip on the train.

Flory and Katie arrived at the church the same time as Peter , he helped them from the carriage, Flory held Peter's arm and he lead her into the church where a lot of the front pews where full. He then got Flory and Katie a seat on the sixth row back . They were very happy sitting so near to the front.

Peter and Joseph both made their way to the front and stood in the Isle waiting for hisbeloved Sarah to arrive.

He turned to Joseph and asked, "just check your pocket please to make sure you have the ring safe.yes Peter of course I will." He checked his pocket, then the other one. Both men froze, then Joseph laughed,"yes of course I have it, it's in my inside pocket, I just wanted to see the look on your face.",Peter nudged him on the arm and they started to laugh. Peter turned around, looks at Flory and smiles, she returns a smile.

Outside the church Sarah's carriage arrives being pulled by two white horse's. Around her carriage were al lsorts of beautiful flowers. Governor Peter Foster waves at Sarah and walks over to her carriage. The driver passes down a set of steps to his carriage groom who puts them safely in front of the door so Sarah and Boo can climb out.

The Governor opens the carriage door, puts out his hand takes Sarah's hand and helps her alight from the carriage. She then steps forwards allowing room for Boo to take the Governor's hand and get her out of the carriage. Boo immediately picks up Sarah's train, shook it nice and straight lifted it slightly off the ground so it didn't get dirty,

In to the church they walked. Sarah holding onto Governor Foster arm, followed by her friend Boo holding her train. All three of them stopped at the entrance of the church andwaited for the organist to start playing the wedding song. HERE COMES THE BRIDE.

The organ starts to play then they slowly walk down the aisle towards the altar. Sarah turned her head looking out for her mum but couldn't see her for the large crowds that filled the church .

The Governor took her right up to where Peter was standing and Peter took her hand.

The vicar stepped forwards and spoke to the people congregation.

"Good morning everyone. Thank you all for coming here today to witness the lawful wedding of Doctor Peter KINGSWOOD and Sarah Wright."

The vicar asks the best man. " Sir, do you have the ring that will unite this couple." Hereplies. "I do," and hands the ring to the vicar.

"Firstly I would like to ask, is there any one present here today that might know of any reason why Peter Kingswood and Sarah Wright cannot be married here in this church today." The church remains quiet.

The vicar carries on, "Do you Doctor Peter Kingswood take thee Sarah Wright to be your lawfully wedded wife? To have and to hold from this day forwards? For better, for worse, for richer or poorer? In sickness and in health, as long as you shall both live?"

Doctor Peter replies, "I DO."

The vicar turns to Sarah and asks, "Do you Sarah Wright take thee Doctor Peter Kingswood to be your lawful husband? To have and to hold from this day forwards? For better, for worse , for richer or poorer ?In sickness and in health, as long as you both shall live ?"

Sarah stops and looks into the air as if she was miles away. She turned her body, looks at Peter, then walks a few paces down the isle and stops.

She stares into the crowd. Everyone started to look at one another inconfusion, Sarah calls out "mother where are you?" Her mother stands up and smiles back at Sarah. "Please mother, "come to me."

She walks over to Sarah and takes her by the arm. They bothwalk over to where Governor Foster is standing. Sarah asks the Governor, "please may my mother take your arm as I want her to be a part of this." "Of course I will Sarah"

The Governor smiles at Mrs Wright takes her hand and rests it firmly on his arm.

Sarah then walks back to Peter's side and looks into Peter eyes-with a big grin on her face,and says, "yes I do."

The vicar then tells Peter, "sir you may kiss the bride."

At this point everyone starts clapping all their children were jumping up and down with excitement.

Peter and Sarah walk back down the aisle followed by Governor Foster, her mother. and their children.

Everyone was invited back to the house for a lovely party.

THE END,(or is it)

EPILOGUE

WHAT HAPPENED NEXT TEN YEARS ON

Doctor Peter and Sarah both worked hard over the next ten years. They extended their house a couple of times to make more bedrooms and more bathrooms, That way they could home more children over the years and never turn any child away.

They also had three children of their own, two boys and a girl who they brought up with all the orphaned children that came to live with them and enjoyed all muddling in together.

It was a very happy home for all. The orphaned children called Peter father, and Sarah mother.

Claire Marchant got released from her sentence after eight years. She stayed in Australia and married a soldier but remained working with the children and Sarah.

George and Boo, after some years left the home, George got new work in Bendigo Hospice and also had two children.

Nurse Linda carried on working at the hospital in Sydney till she retired. She never married, and stayed very good friends with both Peter and Sarah

THE END